T0334639

Cambridge Elements ≡

Elements in Poetry and Poetics
edited by
Eric Falci
University of California, Berkeley

SOMEWHERE ELSE IN THE MARKET

An Essay on the Poetry of J. H. Prynne

Joe Luna
University of Surrey

CAMBRIDGE
UNIVERSITY PRESS

CAMBRIDGE
UNIVERSITY PRESS

Shaftesbury Road, Cambridge CB2 8EA, United Kingdom

One Liberty Plaza, 20th Floor, New York, NY 10006, USA

477 Williamstown Road, Port Melbourne, VIC 3207, Australia

314–321, 3rd Floor, Plot 3, Splendor Forum, Jasola District Centre,
New Delhi – 110025, India

103 Penang Road, #05–06/07, Visioncrest Commercial, Singapore 238467

Cambridge University Press is part of Cambridge University Press & Assessment,
a department of the University of Cambridge.

We share the University's mission to contribute to society through the pursuit of
education, learning and research at the highest international levels of excellence.

www.cambridge.org
Information on this title: www.cambridge.org/9781009345040

DOI: 10.1017/9781009345019

First published 2023

A catalogue record for this publication is available from the British Library.

ISBN 978-1-009-34504-0 Paperback
ISSN 2752-5236 (online)
ISSN 2752-5228 (print)

Cambridge University Press & Assessment has no responsibility for the persistence
or accuracy of URLs for external or third-party internet websites referred to in this
publication and does not guarantee that any content on such websites is, or will
remain, accurate or appropriate.

Somewhere Else in the Market

An Essay on the Poetry of J. H. Prynne

Elements in Poetry and Poetics

DOI: 10.1017/9781009345019
First published online: August 2023

Joe Luna
University of Surrey

Author for correspondence: Joe Luna, josephalexluna@googlemail.com

Abstract: This Element develops a close reading of 'Britain's leading late modernist poet', J. H. Prynne. Examining the political and literary contexts of Prynne's work of the 1980s, the Element offers an intervention into the existing scholarship on Prynne through close attention to the ways in which his poems respond to the social and political forces that define both modern Britain and the wider world of financialized capitalism.

Keywords: poetry, late modernism, modernism, English literature, J. H. Prynne

ISBNs: 9781009345040 (PB), 9781009345019 (OC)
ISSNs: 2752-5236 (online), 2752-5228 (print)

Contents

1 For the Future   1

2 Philological Collage   6

3 Audible Visions   20

4 Strangled Songs   35

5 Somewhere Else   55

References   62

Mao said relinquish space to gain multiplicity of time

—Allen Fisher

1 For the Future

The poetry of J. H. Prynne is not for everybody. In one specific sense, it is not for anybody. The dedication in Prynne's 2015 *Poems* reads 'For the Future'; it replaces the dedications in earlier editions of *Poems* to Prynne's friends, the French poet and translator of Prynne's poetry Bernard Dubourg (1999), and the American poet Edward Dorn (2005). One way to read the 2015 dedication would be to read it in contradiction with the dedications that it replaced and to infer from the substitution of personal connections for a capitalized abstract noun that Prynne intends (at least since 2015) his authorship to stand not in relation to people but to something beyond or apart from them. The idea that Prynne's poetry eschews readers – either in favour of a small group of sycophants and self-appointed cognoscenti or altogether, through a wilfully obscure linguistic hermeticism – has become an established feature of his reception to such a degree that acknowledgement of its influence is now an equally established feature of defences, explanations, and critical exegeses of the work. The charge that Prynne writes poetry the 'purpose' of which is 'to be difficult', and thereby to arrogantly refuse, evade, or simply be incapable of readerly interpretation, has taken on, over the last twenty years, a tone of antagonism markedly more aggressive than the English literary establishment's run-of-the-mill antipathy towards complex forms of literary experimentation.[1] Prynne, it is claimed, 'has been careful to restrict his readership and hide his influence'.[2] 'At one stage', reads a parodic summary of Prynne's career, 'as if fearing a lapse into intelligibility, he actually started writing in Chinese'.[3] Prynne's own statements about his work have likely helped to provoke this kind of reaction. In an oft-quoted letter to the poet Peter Riley in 1985, Prynne wrote that his 'aspiration' has been 'to establish relations not personally with the reader, but with the world and its layers of shifted but recognisable usages; and thereby with the reader's own position within this world.'[4] Prynne's most explicit published reply to the attacks on his writing is a brief aside in the 2007 lecture-essay 'Mental Ears and Poetic Work':

> I am rather frequently accused of having more or less altogether taken leave
> of discernible sense. In fact I believe this accusation to be more or less true,
> and not to me alarmingly so, because what for so long has seemed the arduous

---

[1] Raine, 'All Jokes Aside'.   [2] Mullan, 'Prynne's Progress'.
[3] Ibid. Mullan refers to Prynne's 1992 poem *Jie ban mi Shi Hu*. See Prynne, *Poems*, 379–80.
[4] Quoted in Hall, *On Violence in the Work of J. H. Prynne*, 1.

royal road into the domain of poetry ('what does it mean?') seems less and less an unavoidably necessary precondition for successful reading.[5]

Such replies are hardly likely (or, for that matter, intended) to reconcile Prynne's detractors to his work. They are much more likely to further incense those for whom his poetry is either an elaborate inside joke or the ramblings of a deluded solipsist. The accusations Prynne refers to have only sharpened in the intervening years: in 2016, the *TLS* dubbed him 'the magus of incomprehensibility'.[6] The authors of these claims seem not to be persuaded, by the swathes of published critical interpretations of Prynne's poetry from the 1960s to the present day, that his is a poetry with one of the most dedicated readerships in contemporary literature.[7] When this attention is acknowledged, it emboldens, rather than mollifies, the attacks on Prynne, since the archive of interpretation is received only as further evidence of the merely intellectual snobbery with which his poems are privately consumed by an insular circle of devotees.

The seething derisions of Prynne's comprehensibility in the national print media respond, then, at least in part, to the ways in which the value of his work has been identified and championed by those with access to academic-professional channels of circulation and who are therefore inclined to read and evaluate Prynne's work according to the trends and standards of aesthetic contemplation. Prynne criticism has produced studies that examine the significance of his work in terms of twentieth- and twenty-first-century cultural production, situating it in relation to modernism, late modernism, and postmodernism and arguing for its relevance to any number of critical-theoretical, conceptual, and philosophical criteria of understanding, from postcolonialism to ecocriticism. It has also produced penetrating and incisive accounts of the poetry's literary heritage, contexts, and ideological preoccupations, both in terms of the inheritance of modernist form and style and in terms of the cross-currents of Anglo-American literary exchange and experimentation in the 1960s, as well as close readings of individual poems that evaluate and theorize the work's formal innovations. But even at its most penetrating and incisive, this criticism has often declined to offer accounts of the poetry that situate its critical

---

[5] Prynne, 'Mental Ears and Poetic Work', 132. Whilst it will be clear from what follows that I consider 'successful' reading of Prynne's work to include asking 'what it means', it should be noted that the phonologically oriented reading strategies suggested in 'Mental Ears' (see Section 5), published a decade before the opening of Prynne's archive, prefigure the extremely para-syntactical and sonically modulated lexical constellations that characterize his poetry of the last few years. It seems not unlikely that the reading strategies explored in 'Mental Ears' constituted for Prynne an early hypothesis about the possibilities of the kind of poetic composition that has informed and enabled such a prolific output as he has maintained since 2018.

[6] J. C., 'Little Read Books'.

[7] A bibliography of work written by and about Prynne can be found at https://prynnebibliography .org.

and political motivations in relation to the historical contexts of its author's lifetime. This has led to Prynne's poetry becoming an attractive object of attention from an academic research and publishing culture that thrives on the distribution and application of literary examples to theoretical concepts, at the expense of the perhaps more prosaic work of pointing out when such-and-such a poem was written, what was going on in the world at the time, and what the poetry has to say about its historical moment. Despite its breadth and insight, Prynne criticism has paid scant attention to the historical and political contexts of the poetry, and this interpretative vacancy has made it easier for those critics who wish to do so to throw up their hands in incredulous bafflement and pretend that whatever meaning Prynne's work has is shrouded in the peer-reviewed, rarefied mysteries of the latest in academic literary criticism. One recent study of Prynne's poetry, for example, asserts that the sequence *Not-You* (1993) 'generates an infinite number of readings', a claim whose stylish hyperbole practically invites the impatient cries of fraudulence that may be imagined emanating from the back pages of the *TLS* in reply.

In what follows, I do not seek to convince Prynne's detractors of the value of his work or to claim that its value is located in the very flight from 'discernible sense' that is the object of critical ire and – in the 2007 essay quoted earlier in this section, at least – authorial pride alike. Those readers who believe that there is nothing of interest – let alone pleasure or stimulation – in Prynne's work will almost certainly remain unconvinced by my reading. But literary criticism that claims a universal appeal is no good to anyone. Rather than seek to persuade anyone that they should read Prynne, or to reassure his existing readers that they have been right all along, I seek to supplement the existing readings of his work with an emphasis on the national, political, and economic contexts of the poetry, through close attention to two collections Prynne published in the 1980s. Theoretical elaboration is not absent from my analysis, but I invoke such theory in order to flesh out the historically informed readings herein, rather than to refer the poems to a conceptual arsenal that would justify their value and defend, rather than interpret, their complexity. In doing so, I develop an interpretation of the work that supports an alternative reading of the dedication in the 2015 *Poems* to that which would understand it only in terms of Prynne's desire to 'restrict his readership', or to abandon readers altogether in favour of abstract concepts. In my reading, what 'For the Future' means is inextricable from the poetry's engagement with its historical moment as one in which futures are conceived, constructed, and accomplished entirely within the ideological and economic remit of late, and latterly, of financialized capitalism. Far from being against or antagonistic towards its (or any) readers, Prynne's poetry is 'For the Future' because it positively enjoins readers to identify and self-consciously occupy the same world that poems are capable of knowing, contesting, and resisting, a world in common that is perpetually dissolving into the abstract solution of everyday unfreedom before it resolidifies into the immiserating greed and moral catastrophes of the next bout of imperialist aggression, corporate dehumanization, or the same, seemingly endless, Tory government. From the 1960s to the present day, Prynne's poems bear the scars of their materialist conviction that language and language use are deeply entrenched in, inflected by, and responsive to the reality which they mediate and which is mediated by them. Their experiments, from the playfully anarchic to the arduously philological, thus respond quite earnestly to the Maoist principle, approvingly quoted in Prynne's correspondence, that 'If you want to gain knowledge you must participate in the practice of changing reality', without ever siphoning their energies into revolutionary polemic.[8] 'For the Future' is more militant rallying cry than it is evidence of any post- or anti-humanist resignation: it is a slogan – latterly adopted but retrospectively apt – for the poetry's essential motivation towards a knowledge of the human condition as it is historically, but not, as I shall argue, exhaustively, defined and delimited by every exploitative structure and imperialist legacy in which we live. This motivation is given its most exposed expression in Prynne's poems of the 1980s.

In the last few years, Prynne's *oeuvre* has become 'For the Future' in another, more practical sense. In 2018, Prynne's archive of papers and correspondence, held in Cambridge University Library, was opened to the public. The archive contains an extraordinary amount of material pertaining to the composition of Prynne's poems from the 1960s to very nearly the present day, as well as reams of correspondence with friends, poets, and publishers. Prynne's papers join a trove of archival material collected by the library as part of a project to document, in the library's words, 'papers of poets associated with the so-called "Cambridge School", a term of disputed legitimacy which, when accepted, is often taken to denote both a component of the British Poetry Revival of the 1960s and '70s and a nexus of late-modernist writers'.[9] The Cambridge poetry archives contain the papers of some of the poets with whom Prynne developed into maturity through conversation, correspondence, and continual exchange, including some associated with the privately circulated poetry worksheet *The English Intelligencer* in the mid-1960s, such as David Chaloner, Andrew Crozier, Jeremy Hilton, John James, and Peter Riley. The archive also includes

---

[8] Mao, *An Anthology of His Writings*, 205. Prynne quotes Mao's advice in a letter to Douglas Oliver, 23 October 1991. MS Add.10144, J. H. Prynne Papers, University of Cambridge Library.
[9] Cambridge University Library, 'Cambridge School Poets'.

papers of Prynne's contemporaries or near-contemporaries whose names evoke varying degrees of association with the 'Cambridge School', such as Anthony Barnett, Michael Haslam, Tom Raworth, Denise Riley, and John Riley. The archive represents, in part, the papers and correspondence of a community of poets that scholarship has only just begun to account for and interpret.

Prynne's papers reveal that he assembled and preserved files of photocopies, newspaper clippings, articles, and various other textual source materials, specifically relating to almost every collection of poems he wrote and published since the 1960s. Such assembly and preservation speak both to Prynne's compositional practice and to his sense of the legacy of that practice. What does it say about Prynne's poetry that he has actively sought, late in his life, to encourage public access to the textual source materials of the vast majority of his writing output of the last half a century, materials that he has assiduously collated over the course of his career but which have remained out of reach to most of his readers until very recently? Speculation on Prynne's authorial motivations might raise any number of possible answers to this question, and I will here restrict myself to what seem to me to be the two most likely. The most immediately plausible answer is that Prynne conceives of the archival materials as part of the work of poetry that produces, but is not therefore terminated by, finished poems; or at least, that finished poems are an ongoing negotiation with their source materials that require an understanding of the language base they draw upon for their spirit of philological enquiry to be properly historicized. On these terms, the opening of the archive is a late invitation to readers to study the sources and local inspirations for the poems, the better to understand both their immediate contexts and the ways in which they attempt to interrogate or transcend these contexts. In my response to this invitation, I seek less to divine Prynne's conception of poetical labour than to read the poems themselves. Another answer to the question of Prynne's motivations in opening the archive has to do with the relationships between his work and that of his contemporaries more generally, represented by the papers of those above-named poets (and others) held in Cambridge and by sundry other archival collections of papers and manuscripts, including (to name only a few) those of Edward Dorn, Barry MacSweeney, Anna Mendelssohn, Douglas Oliver, and Charles Olson. The opening of Prynne's archives puts the sources of his work – textual, inspirational, and epistolary – amongst the publicly held archives of poets with and through whom Prynne's poetic practice has developed over the course of his life.

Whatever the answers given to the question posed above, it is difficult not to discern in the opening of Prynne's archive a certain strain of authorial anxiety about the work's reception since 2018, whether in the form of a defensive riposte to the accusations of 'incomprehensibility' (as if Prynne were saying, 'attend to these texts/objects and you'll see what I mean') or as a more selfless, though no less anxious, indication of a process of social sense-making that is essential to any poetic community (as if Prynne were saying, 'comprehension of any one poet is indissociable from the ways in which that poet develops through constant exchange with others, both living and dead; here's my contribution'). Prynne's poetry is a difficult poetry, not just by comparison with any given Craig Raine or Don Paterson but in relation to the most extreme experimenta-tions in language, syntax, and form of the last century, and Prynne criticism has discussed and explored the poetry's complexity in this sense again and again, with varying degrees of success. Yet the poetry's 'purpose' could only be said 'to be difficult' and 'difficult' alone if the sole motivation for, and intellectual origin of, its composition was a practically infantile desire to obscure and confuse. The opening of Prynne's archive does not suggest that his poems have been unreadable until now any more than the opening of any literary archive abolishes the significance of earlier interpretations of the author's work. Prynne's papers, like most literary archives, do not contain written summaries or explanation of any of his poems. But they do contain a wealth of material that clarifies the work's contexts, intertexts, and subtexts, and they offer, as a result, innumerable avenues of interpretation to supplement the existing scholarship. The entire Cambridge poetry archive provides a welcome opportunity to deepen our understanding of a hugely various community of writers, many of whom found in Prynne's work a consistently vital and exploratory example. It seems very likely that to maintain henceforth that Prynne's poems are the arcana of a kooky hermeticism will begin to sound uncannily like an obscurantist fantasy, one that not only deliberately decontextualizes the poetry from the entire history of modernist literature but also fraudulently decouples it from the world in which all poems, and all criticism, gets written. What follows is a reading of Prynne's poetry very much in sight of the world in which it was written.

2 Philological Collage

One of the great contributions to Prynne scholarship of Richard Kerridge and the late N. H. Reeve's annotated edition of *The Oval Window* ([1983] 2018) is Kerridge's emphasis on collage as a compositional principle of the poem, and indeed of Prynne's entire *oeuvre*.[10] Kerridge notes that since 'the

---

[10] Prynne, *The Oval Window: A New Annotated Edition* (hereafter cited as *TOW*).

1968 publication of *Kitchen Poems* ... a fundamental component of Prynne's poetry has been the use of lines quoted from different sources, literary, scientific and otherwise technical, without the mediation of a dramatic speaker'.[11] No reader who has spent any time with Prynne's poetry could fail to notice quite how fundamental this aspect of the work is. As Kerridge and Reeve show by reference to the materials preserved by Prynne and held in his archive, some of the poems in *The Oval Window* are stuffed with quotation and part-quotation to such an extent that such material visibly constitutes a major part – if not the majority – of their content. This is the sixth poem in *The Oval Window*'s sequence of twenty-seven:

> Somewhere else in the market it's called
> a downward sell-out, to get there first
> and cut open a fire break. Less won't do,
> more isn't on either. How a gang of boys
> set her face alight with a flaming aerosol can,
> "her mouth was sealed up by the burns."
> Attention is low in historic terms and will
> drift down, seeming to falter slowly and
> making excuses for the money numbers ahead.[12]

The poem is at least as much arranged as it is composed, using modified text from *The Times* and *The Financial Times* newspapers of 22–25 August 1983. Despite the first line's straightforward grammar of narrative continuity, the poem does not straightforwardly pick up and continue a narrative from the previous poem/s in the sequence. The line is the first to introduce the (retrospective) suggestion that the subject of any or all of the preceding five poems should be considered 'in' such terms, as if we had been there, 'in the market', all along, and the poems had been working to establish or describe whatever 'it' is; the empty subject of 'it's' accentuates the uncanny suggestion of an established familiarity through a phraseology familiar from colloquial usage (e.g., 'it's going to rain'). The phrase 'downward sell-out' is adjusted by Prynne from 'downward spiral', as it appears in a market round-up in *The Times* (25 August 1983), 'Shareholders fear 1984'. The adjustment substitutes the specific jargon of liquidation and brokerage ('sell-out') for the report's more general indication of a market slump ('spiral').[13] The following clause implies, in the grammar of further clarification, that the 'sell-out' is not only fraught with competition but inherently desirous and that to 'cut open a firebreak' is the desired privilege of whoever 'get[s] there first'. The word 'firebreak' is split in two (it is 'cut open'), as if to conjure the image of a broken vacancy, an empty

---

[11] Ibid., 10.   [12] Ibid., 41.   [13] Lintott, 'Shareholders Fear 1984', 14.

space further dirempted; 'fire' also makes the desired end of the 'sell-out'
descriptively coeval with the anecdote of extreme violence in lines 4–6. 'Less
won't do, / more isn't on either' is couched in the grammar of idiomatic or
proverbial speech: it audibly negates and then unfolds the proverbial 'less is
more' into a doubly negative equivocation, as if extruding a sound-bite justification for Thatcherite state retrenchment generally, and cutbacks to the National
Health Service and unemployment benefit in particular, through a quantitative
double bind. A small report on the front page of *The Times* (22 August 1983)
provides the material for 'How a gang of boys / set her face alight with a flaming
aerosol can, / "her mouth was sealed up by the burns"', which, despite the
special fidelity to source material implied by the quotation marks around
'her mouth . . .', is almost all quoted verbatim.[14] The single adjustment to the
report's text is 'boys' for the original's 'skinheads' – in this instance, the
alteration serves to universalize rather than particularize the found material,
so that those capable of such injury are not delimited by their appearance but
named so as to evoke developmental continuity with 'men' more generally.[15]

The poem ends with text adapted from three sentences from two reports in
The Financial Times of 24–25 August 1983, quoted in Kerridge and Reeve's
edition as such: 'Profits are expected to remain low, in historic terms',
'Improvement in export performance next year is predicted on the assumptions
that sterling will drift lower', and 'Last year, however, the Fed[eral Reserve]
was frightened almost out of its wits by the impending foreign debt crisis; to
save the banking system it adopted a new point of forcing interest rates down,
and making excuses for the money numbers.'[16] The substitution of 'Attention'
for 'Profits' in the seventh line translates the subsequent description of financial
market dynamics ('low in historic terms') into a faculty of consciousness
('Attention'), as well as implying this consciousness's ambivalent relationship
to the violence transcribed in lines 4–6. The poem's last line is a proleptic
counterpart to the first line's grammar of retrospection: in addition to being one
of three verb phrases belonging to the subject 'Attention' – as if attention itself
were capable of abdicating responsibility – 'making excuses for the money
numbers ahead' also reads, by punning on 'numbers' in the sense of verses, as
a metatextual indication of the monetarist and financial subject matter in the
twenty-one poems to come ('money numbers'). Newspaper clippings and faux-
idiomatic speech provide the major linguistic objects of the collage; their
alteration and arrangement splice together specimens of human orientation,
desire, violence, and attention with the spatial and temporal logics of international financial markets.

---

[14] Horsnell, 'Threat to Baby in 6p Mugging', 1.   [15] Ibid.   [16] *TOW*, 99.

The most convincing accounts of Prynne's poetry yet produced all address the shifting rhetorical and discursive bricolage of the poems and its implications. Kerridge writes that '[c]ollage of this kind [in *The Oval Window*] is clearly a device for breaking boundaries and disrupting cultural niches, so as to bring together discourses normally kept separate (literary, scientific, medical, financial, technological'.[17] Justin Katko argues that 'The *Plant Time Manifold* Transcripts' (in *Wound Response* (1974)) 'smears the boundaries which render discontinuous not only poetry and modern science but the scientific disciplines themselves' and suggests that the 'radical philological method [therein] practiced is perhaps a metonym for the reorganisation of all available means of knowing, along ethical, aesthetic, and logical axes'.[18] Ryan Dobran, discussing the poems of the 1970s, characterizes Prynne's style as 'a scalpel of research into the scientific image of genetics, relativistic cosmology, molecular biology, pharmacology, and the plant sciences'.[19] Keston Sutherland's readings of 'L'Extase de M. Poher' (in *Brass* (1971)) establish the relationship between knowledge and power in *Brass* and beyond in the following terms: '[k]nowledge cut adrift from power is ... locked beneath a deflective screen of bathos; yet it remains knowledge', surviving, in the case of 'L'Extase', in the poem's 'grids that destroy the integrity of syntax and expository argument' but produce what Sutherland (elsewhere) calls 'unity by default and coercion' and '*lyric as text* harassed into ... totality'.[20] And Lisa Jeschke, in her reading of 'the ruin considered as a rubbish product of history' in *Unanswering Rational Shore* (2001), implicitly develops Sutherland's argument into a reading of the late work's 'dense, broken, difficult language' as part of the work's uptake of a 'political necessity [to acknowledge] the ruined reality of words in an age of accelerated communication'.[21] Kerridge's emphasis on collage, especially collage considered as 'Modernist poetic [form]', suggests a methodological continuum across Prynne's *oeuvre* that helpfully connects these strands of scholarship and commentary.[22] Each of them articulates something of the work's consistent unification of disparate strands of textual meaning and music to produce poems that challenge the epistemological foundations of modernity and modern capitalism.

Anthony Mellors and Ryan Dobran have both used the term 'philological collage' to describe Prynne's early contribution to *The English Intelligencer*, 'A Pedantic Note in Two Parts', a term which neatly encapsulates that text's assembly and appearance, viz. 'a collage of cut-and-pasted elements from

---

[17] Ibid., 14.   [18] Katko, 'Relativistic Phytosophy', 250.

[19] Dobran, 'The Difficult Style', 161.

[20] Sutherland, 'J. H. Prynne and Philology', 246; Sutherland, 'Hilarious Absolute Daybreak', 147.

[21] Jeschke, 'Late Early Poetry', 61, 70.   [22] *TOW*, 12.

academic texts, along with hand-written commentary'.[23] But Kerridge's ascription of collage to Prynne's broader practice presents the opportunity to read Mellors' and Dobran's characterizations of 'A Pedantic Note' as part of a continuous predilection for collage form and the ways in which it is put to use across Prynne's writing, whether as literal xeroxed assemblage in correspondence, the interleaving of literary, scientific, medical, financial, or newsprint quotation or information in the poems, or as the syncretism of nominally discrete orders of human understanding as general poetic *praxis*. The attentions and objects of Prynnian collage in the 1980s, as the foregoing reading of 'Somewhere else in the market . . .' has already suggested, must be read in the context of Thatcherite Britain's programme of state and social recomposition, including privatization, the piecemeal dismantling of the welfare state, and the deregulation of the banks and financial markets.[24] The poems of this period become more collaged than ever before in response to changes in the economy and political landscape that have since become hallmarks of what is called financialization and its ideological 'umbrella', neoliberalism.[25] They respond to both the ethos of these changes and to the 'profound technical change[s] in information processing and telecommunications' since the 1970s that facilitated, amongst other things, the shift from open outcry on the floor of the London Stock Exchange to a digital, screen-based market.[26] The poems become more and more composed from pieces of textual material the more the welfare state is taken to pieces; their meaning rests more and more on the variety of connections shared by their sources the more the figure of the shareholder becomes the economic, ethical, and ideological idol of the United Kingdom; and they rely more and more on the deployment and arrangement of actual newsprint the more the circulation of information becomes more crucial to the market than the currency standards that underpinned pre-1971 global finance.[27]

Collage has long been recognized as one of the defining aesthetic practices of the twentieth century and disjunction, fragmentation, and parataxis long understood as the aesthetic correlates of an age of mass consumption, alienation, and decolonization. Prynne's intensified collage production in the 1980s joins a long and varied lineage of modernist practice in assemblage stretching back to the

---

[23] Mellors, *Late Modernist Poetics*, 130; Dobran, 'The Difficult Style', 52; Pattison, Pattison, and Roberts, eds., *Certain Prose of The English Intelligencer*, xxxi.

[24] The term 'authoritarian populism' is Stuart Hall's; see *The Hard Road to Renewal*, 42: 'What we have to explain is a move toward "authoritarian populism" – an exceptional form of the capitalist state which, unlike classical fascism, has retained most (though not all) of the formal representative institutions in place, and which at the same time has been able to construct around itself an active popular consent.'

[25] See Lapavitsas, *Profiting without Producing*, 172.   [26] Ibid.

[27] See Vogl, *The Specter of Capital*, 77.

turn of the twentieth century, legible across the arts, from Picasso to Robert Duncan to Stan Brakhage. There is, furthermore, a discernible collective turn towards a specifically poetical collage practice by several of Prynne's close contemporaries in the 1980s, a turn galvanized by the rapid expansion of commercially available technologies of reproduction. Allen Fisher, Barry MacSweeney, Anna Mendelssohn, Douglas Oliver, Maggie O'Sullivan, and Tom Raworth each develop more-or-less collage-based practices in the period – whether literal (i.e., frequent use of quoted text, with or without attribution), paratactical (i.e., utilizing a grammar of intense disjunction and fragmentation), or both – and each draws on various strands of modernist, Dadaist, and surrealist practice to do so, as do contemporaries in North America such as Charles Bernstein, Susan Howe, and Steve McCaffery. Allen Fisher's seminal work of late modernist assemblage, *Brixton Fractals* (1985), for example, combines Blakean vision, situationist *dérive*, and catastrophe theory in a study of the physical, architectural, and affective discontinuities of contemporary urban space. Its poems are composed through incessant quotation of, and reference to, a huge variety of source material, from Adorno to Zeeman, through which is produced a febrile, alchemical, and neo-constructivist image of the capital. Whilst Fisher's collage practice mines literary and scientific history for its poems' component parts, Barry MacSweeney's *Colonel B* (1980) subjects the poet's earlier work to a textual reconstitution that is both authorial self-examination and apocalyptic satire of Tory rule. Luke Roberts argues that *Colonel B*, 'littered with quotations from the poet's earlier work' as it is, 'becomes more densely allusive than anything [MacSweeney] had written before. Every line seems to contain a hidden meaning or secret, leaving the reader in a perpetual state of suspicion.'[28] Roberts further suggests that the poem's transactional dynamism, constantly swapping back and forth between texts and voices, is written in deranged, burlesque imitation of faith in the free market 'as the animating force of all human life'.[29]

Prynne's work of the 1980s, like MacSweeney's of the late 1970s and early 1980s, develops in response to Thatcherite market idolatry. Practically every book Prynne published between 1968 and 2011 makes overt or implicit reference to the world of modern finance, but the 'restoration of capitalist imperatives through the application of unmodified market principles' under Thatcher and financialization's coordination of 'the life of the social body with the movement of capital' are the central foci of the poetry in the 1980s.[30]

---

[28] See Roberts, *Barry MacSweeney and the Politics of Post-War British Poetry*, 116–17.
[29] Ibid., 121.
[30] Hall, *The Hard Road to Renewal*, 59; Vogl, *The Specter of Capital*, 102. For Prynne's 1989 sequence *Word Order*, readers are referred to John Wilkinson's essay on the poem, 'Heigh Ho:

The original publication dates of *The Oval Window* and *Bands around the Throat* straddle the 1986 'Big Bang' reform of the British financial sector. The former offers glimpses of the self as, by turns, a privatized economy and a financialized interiority and positions its shifting portrait of this subject as the contested site of Thatcherite ideology. In its second half, *The Oval Window* fashions a synaesthetic fantasy of lyric tranquillity, a fantasy which promptly collapses back into the daily grind of Thatcherite Britain. *Bands around the Throat*, meanwhile, is a post–Big Bang collection: it is more directly concerned than *The Oval Window* with financial markets and their technical infrastructures, though still in relation to Thatcherite political power. In *Bands around the Throat*, there is no room for an excursion through a vision of tranquil alterity, however compromised and short-lived, and its flashes of traditional song and nursery rhyme are poised between bathos and lamentation; yet they remain the echoes, however faint, of a popular speech still capable of an affective register beyond fear and despair. The litter of quotations that comprises so much of these books, as I explore in what follows, leads the reader not so much into a 'state of suspicion', as Roberts suggests of MacSweeney's work, but down into the rhetorical and associative hinterlands of their sources. Quotation in Prynne's 1980s work is collaged into consequence and continuity by a versification of incessant re-presentation of various orders of literary, political, and economic significance, so that the cumulative economy of the poetic object (in Sutherland's terms, its harassed or coerced totality) traces a legible seam across those very orders of knowledge. It is in this sense that Prynne's poems are properly philological collages. They survey the profound enmeshment of human life within and across the systemic abundance of false needs and ethical redundancy that are native to a developed capitalist society, and in doing so they seek to produce their own anti-systems of lexical and historical relationships. Philological collage as practised by Prynne is thus a method of making knowledge obstreperously, antagonistically, appear.

But what kind of knowledge, exactly? In much of Prynne's work of the 1960s, the knowledge native to poetry, and which it is the special preserve of poetic numbers to enumerate and amplify, is essentially knowledge of our capacity for ontological and phenomenological self-possession in the face of the ubiquitous alienation from our true selves that is encouraged by the commercial, imperial, and financial world order. The '*moralism* of immediate knowledge', as Sutherland puts it, is coincident in Prynne's early work with our sensuous and affective experience of it; it is felt, in Wordsworthian

---

A Partial Gloss of *Word Order*'. Wilkinson's brilliant gloss of the many song lyrics collaged into the sequence plainly rhymes with the claims I make about *The Oval Window* and *Bands around the Throat*.

sympathy, in the blood, and along the heart: 'I am moved,' Prynne writes in *The White Stones* (1969), 'by the *condition* of knowledge, as the / dispersal of form', a condition most fully sounded out in the form of the verse that shapes this very claim.[31] Knowledge of this kind in the early work is subtly but surely distinguished from the kind of knowledge exemplified by the bureaucratic infrastructures and political ideologies of a developed capitalist state and market economy, just as the Augustinian 'city of love' is distinguished from the land of electoral politics and the 'intangible consumer networks' it resembles.[32] Poetic knowledge, founded on the philological desire for a unified totality of mankind, promises in this early work nothing less than a kind of secular paradise. But it does not promise it for long. As Sutherland and others have shown, the breakdown of the proposed ultimate coherence of what we know and who we are is the generative crisis of Prynne's poetry of the 1970s and beyond, that which impels the head-on collision with the data of contemporary alienation and the 'unwitty circus' of political spectacle as a means of ascertaining precisely who and where we are, a kind of knowing which is instantiated by the satirical and bathos-drenched 1971 collection *Brass*. This shift of emphasis is manifested through an increasing reliance on collage as a compositional technique.

For post-*Brass* Prynne the Maoist dialectician, poetic knowledge is no more the inalienably radical essence of ontological coherence than it is a false idol of bourgeois idealism. That no purity of essentially human knowledge is native to poetry does not eliminate but intensifies poetry's capacity to radically concentrate and heighten our experience of the contexts of knowing into which we are born and which shape our capacity for thought and reflection. The knowledge produced by philological collage is knowledge inseparable from the complex of ideological, political, and economic forces through which we act, which act upon us, and which open up and constrain the horizons of political and social life at large. In this sense, the knowledge to be gained by reading a poem might as well be got from reading anything else, perhaps especially critical, theoretical, or journalistic explanations of politics or society. But poetry is also qualitatively differentiated from these other kinds of thinking and knowing by its capacity to concentrate specimens of thought and knowledge within the bounds of a single line or phrase, and indeed to break, interrupt, and contradict them in the same breath. The phrase 'Attention is low in historic terms' makes a faculty of cognition coincident with economic downturn, suggesting that economic depression makes people less aware of the wider economic forces

---

[31] Sutherland, 'Hilarious Absolute Daybreak', 115; Prynne, *Poems*, 78.

[32] Sutherland, 'Hilarious Absolute Daybreak', 115; Prynne, *Poems*, 14.

shaping their lives (because they are more immediately concerned with paying the rent); it also encourages the power of attention (such as the reader's) to disclose the 'historic' nature of the economic contexts doing the shaping. The radical economy of poetic form becomes for Prynne in the 1970s and 1980s a place of embattled disclosure, not of authentic human being but of the logics and technologies of late capitalism – from privatization to the screen market – that reorient what the social body means for capital and of how this reorientation both disables some and enables other ways of knowing ourselves and the world in which we live. Specifically poetic knowledge, then, becomes for Prynne knowledge *of* the dialectical relationship between what we know (or don't know) and how we know it (or don't know it), from the thresholds of the physical and neurological in *Wound Response* (1974) to the behavioural and ideological ramifications of Thatcherism explored in *The Oval Window* and *Bands around the Throat*. Each of these books encounters the world as a complex of oppressive and coercive forces, and in doing so they seek both to know that world and to manufacture, through their formal disposition as philological collage, a kind of epistemological sabotage of the ideological coherence of those forces.

An important literary precursor to the collage form developed by Prynne in the 1980s – as on the development of collage into a touchstone of modernist sensibility more generally – is that of the *Cantos* of Ezra Pound. The importance of Pound's influence on Prynne throughout his career is well established, especially in the work of Latter, Mellors, and Sutherland. Sutherland's account strongly suggests that, whilst Prynne, in correspondence with Olson in the 1960s, censures Pound's 'sacralised ignorance' (by which he means Pound's abrasive disdain for detailed historical, scientific, and textual research), he maintains a strong and productive connection to Pound's work that lasts well beyond his break with Olson.[33] This suggestion is borne out in particular with regard to the 1980s work by a reference on the first page of *The Oval Window* to Pound's *Cantos* that draws attention to the collage method of that earlier work. The opening poem of *The Oval Window* contains the line-broken clause 'at a loss / for two-ply particles / set callow', in which 'two-ply particles' recalls the phrase 'Ply over ply', a repeated motif in Pound, notably in Canto IV, where it is part of the vivid description of 'The liquid and rushing crystal / beneath the knees of the gods' in the Canto's impression of paradise.[34] As Kerridge points out, Pound's phrase also offers a summary description of the cumulative/

---

[33] Prynne, 'A Letter to Andrew Duncan', 102.

[34] Or 'Ovidian Eden': see Dekker, 'Myth and Metamorphosis', 290; *TOW*, 36; Pound, *The Cantos of Ezra Pound*, 15.

associative collage through which the *Cantos* themselves are composed.[35] That Prynne's poem is, from its very beginning, 'at a loss / for two-ply particles / set callow' suggests two things. First, that the Poundian reliance on the arrangement of an epic architecture of textual fragments to establish a knowledge of human history, ethics, and spiritual paradise is unavailable and undesirable if the fragments in aggregate are presumed to grant direct access to such knowledge ('set callow', followed in the poem, on a new line, by 'set bland and clean', suggests such a treatment of the 'particles' would be unbearably naïve, not to mention simply mistaken). And second, that by acknowledging it is 'at a loss / for two-ply particles / set callow', the poem may instead begin, and proceed, to develop a collage the 'particles' of which will not be 'callow' but emphatically *experienced*, arranged and embedded according to a greater fidelity to the world from which they derive, and to which they refer, than Pound was ever interested in pursuing. This is the method developed in *The Oval Window* and intensified in *Bands around the Throat*. In these books, the collaged fragments discordantly cohere, echoing the literary, cultural, political, economic, and technical institutions from which they derive their histories of meaning. It is through and across these institutions, not despite or beside them, that knowledge is sought, frustrated, and sought again. Prynne's collage method in the 1980s is not designed, as Pound's ultimately was, to discover the knowledge required to inhabit the coherence of a unified social and cultural totality. It is designed, instead, to make poetic knowledge confront, and compete with, the already existing unified totality of the market.

The most consistent and visible component of Prynne's collages of the 1980s is the news. Newsprint suffuses *The Oval Window* and *Bands around the Throat* more than any other textual source material, and whilst it can often retreat from the kind of prominence it has in poems such as 'Somewhere else in the market . . .', it is never far from the language-surface or referential circumference of the poems. Early in his career, in the context of his formative involvement in *The English Intelligencer* circle, Prynne proposed an extraordinary concept of news that would entail 'a new *hold* on the language of this world', through the prosodic and epistemological content of poems that served as the connective tissue of the wished-for community exemplified by the *Intelligencer*'s design and circulation.[36] This concept of news, which is closely connected to Prynne's thinking about the relationship between poetry and knowledge in the mid-late 1960s, and which is deeply opposed to the mediated reflection of worldly events that characterizes traditional newsprint, is abandoned along with the worksheet itself in the late 1960s, as Alex Latter's account

---

[35] See *TOW*, 20.   [36] Quoted in Latter, *Late Modernism and* The English Intelligencer, 87.

of the *Intelligencer*'s collective project has shown.[37] What comes to replace it, and which underlies the later poetry's persistent use of newsprint as a source, is a conviction that such reflection must be sewn into the critical praxis of literary endeavour that seeks a knowledge of the world fully plugged-in to its networks of globalized commerce and political power, relationships to which the reportage in the daily broadsheets provide a running commentary. Newsprint, once effectively considered by some of the *Intelligencer* poets as a debased form of epistemological currency to be opposed and transcended through a form of knowledge distinctly poetical, fraternal, and wishful, becomes for Prynne a persistent element in the composition of poetry that seeks to encounter the world's myriad forms of moral, political, and ideological debasement. Here is another way in which Prynne develops a Poundian poetics through and beyond Pound: whereas Pound claims that 'Literature is news that STAYS news', in order, as one critic puts it, 'to fend off the planned obsolescence accompanying cultural mass production', Prynne's reliance upon, and interpolation of, actual newsprint in his 1980s poems literalizes Pound's dictum according to the inverse of its motivated logic: by incorporating contemporary reportage into the lines of poems in order to refer the very production of contemporaneity and its possible futures to a mass cultural obsolescence.[38] The *Intelligencer* was an attempt to overcome or at least defy this obsolescence and to circulate news of the 'community of wish' that the worksheet strove to articulate.[39] After its demise, the incorporation of newsprint into Prynne's poems reads as a dialectical reversal, or negative fulfilment of that earlier collective project, with the poems themselves now charged with the news they must stay – hold, arrested, within the bounds of the poem – and stay abreast of.

Prynne's relationship to the news of the 1980s is best characterized as a depressively compulsive one. 'You have to believe', he wrote to Edward and Jennifer Dunbar Dorn on 24 February 1985, 'that newsprint is generically hateful to me now, in all forms an addiction which will bring ruin by the naivety of our disgust'.[40] This handwritten letter is photocopied into a collage of clippings from two consecutive days of *The Times* front pages in February 1985. The whole document is arranged so that Prynne's cursive hand sits directly beneath two articles covering Thatcher's trip to Washington, DC that month, and at ninety degrees to another article covering a break in the government talks with the then striking British miners, featuring the prediction by the former asset-stripper and future Kleinwort Benson chairman (then Secretary of State for Energy) Peter Walker that the miners would be back at

---

[37] See Latter, *Late Modernism and* The English Intelligencer, chap. 3.
[38] Cohen, 'Getting Generic', 147–8.   [39] Prynne, *Poems*, 53.
[40] Prynne to the Dorns, 24 February 1985. J. H. Prynne Papers.

work 'within the next few days' (he was right); a fourth story adjacent to the main strike news is visible only by its headline, 'Break in talks pleases Tories'.[41] The substance of Prynne's letter is hemmed in by newsprint columns, headlines, and, in the top-right corner of the page, the cropped image (from the front page of the 21 February edition) of Thatcher giving a speech to the American Congress. Prynne's inset letter-text concludes:

> So few are free who mock their chains, trading on pathos as the slavish joke within a Sunday-school collectivism. The poetry of revolution and everyday life! Here [in the UK] the last twitches of our civil war are being crushed and flushed out for export, while the organ-grinders finish off the Health Service and the last chance for the last in the queue; you scrape the barrel and then the hoop contracts. I read the stories every morning, the front page was a busted flush right the start (enclosed). I did not mean any personal affront but the shock-wave of basic revulsion at even the format is still our daily bread & dripping.[42]

The 'last twitches of our civil war' refers to the dying strike. The 'personal affront' that Prynne 'did not mean' refers to a previous letter to the Dorns, sent a few months earlier. This earlier letter is depressively scathing about the latest issue of the 'literary newspaper' *Rolling Stock*, edited by the Dorns and featuring contributions and reportage from a host of poets, artists, and critics, including Prynne.[43] It is signed off:

> Perhaps the newsprint could be pressed into some more durable employ, like the wrapping for a pack of eucharistic silicon wafers, or the preamble to a comic-cuts version of the next SALT treaty. And perhaps I should keep my mouth shut.[44]

Prynne and the Dorns were great friends and long-time collaborators, and it is a measure of their abiding trust in each other that such caustic disgust is given as free a rein in the correspondence as praise for each other's work – especially when that work's affective mandate is itself a form of disgust: 'Abhorrence seems exactly the correct address', writes Prynne in the (somewhat reparative) February 1985 letter, referring in the singular to the title of Ed Dorn's epigrammatic satires, *Abhorrences*, that he worked on throughout the decade.[45] Prynne's self-confessed 'addiction' to newsprint combines a ravenous daily

---

[41] Routledge, 'Walker Rules Out Talks As Miners Vote to Strike On'; Haviland, 'Break in Talks Pleases Tories', 1.

[42] Prynne to the Dorns, 24 February 1985.

[43] See Dorn, '*Rolling Stock*: A Chronicle of the Eighties', 154. Prynne's contribution is an untitled letter to the editors, dated 7 October 1984; see *Rolling Stock* 8, 2.

[44] Prynne to the Dorns, 18 November 1984. J. H. Prynne Papers.

[45] Prynne to the Dorns, 24 February 1985.

consumption of the news with 'basic revulsion at . . . the format' and a reflexive admonition of the 'naivety' at his own intuitive reaction to what he read. The news he read throughout the 1980s, mostly in *The Times* (but also in *The Financial Times* and the local *Cambridge Evening News*), was dominated by the saga of Tory party assault on (what Thatcher lambasted as) the 'collectivist' approach of the post-war consensus, in order to engineer what Thatcher defined, in opposition to it, as the 'personal society'.[46]

Earlier in the decade, in the wake of Thatcher's landslide 9 June 1983 re-election, Prynne had anticipated (in this instance in correspondence with Ed Dorn alone) that the Conservative political strategy was to be a behavioural tenderization of the British electorate:

> [T]he major 'thrust' of the second term is to be the vast deconstruction of the welfare state, with its expensive support for the lost and strayed. To get hanging and first-strike nuclear capacity talked about by an eager proletariat doesn't mean that either are wanted, exactly; but they soften up the fall-back positions which are to chop unemployment benefit and to privatise most of the health service . . . If a democratic franchise can indeed be worked up to hate criminals with enough righteous fury to want the return of judicious murder, then the sick and workless are lesser targets towards whom the passions of social revenge, baulked of their prime scapegoats, can easily be deflected . . . thus the primal underpinnings, moral and collective, of the welfare state as an attitude of mind, can be destabilised from below via the even more primal motive [*sic*] of fearful retaliation and licensed social hatred.[47]

Prynne's letter refers to specific political debates and agendas during Thatcherism's second wave. On 13 July 1983, a motion to reintroduce capital punishment in the United Kingdom was defeated in the House of Commons by 223 to 368.[48] The previous week, *The Times* reported the government's reiter-ated 'intention to deploy cruise missiles at Greenham Common by the end of the year', in the face of continued protest by the Greenham Common Women's Peace Camp.[49] The letter articulates the political background to *The Oval Window*, the majority of which Prynne composed in the summer of 1983, and which dramatizes the social physiognomy of Thatcherite anti-collectivism, with especial reference to cuts to the National Health Service, unemployment bene-fit, and Treasury policy. It is a disgusted letter, foreshadowing Prynne's despair and 'disgust' two years later at the stories he continued to ingest; it is full of scorn for everybody from 'the Iron Harpy' (Thatcher), to 'women' ('To charge

---

[46] Thatcher, 'Interview for *Sunday Times*'.
[47] Prynne to Dorn, 17 July 1983. J. H. Prynne Papers.
[48] Parliamentary Debates, Commons, 13 July 1983.
[49] Cowton, 'Arms Spending Rises 19% under Tories', 4.

spot cash for blood transfusion would be probably the most advanced coup, with maybe a budget silvertop for the careless who couldn't afford gold. The women would vote for that'), to 'the working class' (who 'pine for romantic conscription and who have been deprived by the trade unions of their natural right to hate the workless').[50]

Prynne's condescension towards the 'eager proletariat' and his casual sexism notwithstanding, his bulletin to Dorn – with its sense of an ascendent 'democratic franchise' engineered to undercut the 'welfare state as an attitude of mind' – is strongly reminiscent of Stuart Hall's 1978 analysis of 'authoritarian populism' and 'populist moralism':

> Neither Keynesianism nor monetarism ... win votes as such in the electoral marketplace. But, in the discourse of 'social market values,' Thatcherism discovered a powerful means of translating economic doctrine into the language of experience, moral imperative and common sense, thus providing a 'philosophy' in the broader sense – an alternative *ethic* to that of the 'caring society'. This translation of a theoretical *ideology* into a populist *idiom* was a major political achievement: and the conversion of hard-faced economics into the language of compulsive *moralism* was, in many ways, the centrepiece of this transformation ... The process we are looking at here is very similar to that which Gramsci once described as *transformism*: the neutralization of some elements in an ideological formation and their absorption and passive appropriation into a new political configuration.[51]

Hall's analysis is sober and strategic; it is as if Prynne's June 1983 letter to Dorn collapses Hall's description of historical-ideological dynamics into a phlegmatic condemnation of both Thatcher's appeal to the 'primal motive[s] of fearful retaliation and licenced social hatred' and those 'motive[s]' themselves. But Hall's sense of Thatcherism's translation of 'economic doctrine into the language of experience, moral imperative and common sense' is nevertheless extremely close to Prynne's appalled rendition of Thatcherism's hegemonic aspirations for the body politic. Monetarism is the economic doctrine, popularized by Milton Friedman and Anna Schwartz in the 1960s, that posited inflation as a 'purely monetary phenomenon [to be] cured by restricting the supply of money', and which thus justified 'raising interest rates ... and cutting state spending to try to lower the Public Sector Borrowing Requirement'.[52] It is identified by Hall and Prynne as the theoretical-ideological backbone of Thatcherism's 'alternative *ethic*', in line with contemporary left-wing analysis of the creed in terms of its justification for national 'attempts to weaken union power, cut and privatize state activity and remove exchange controls ... [and] to

---

[50] Prynne to Dorn, 17 July 1983.   [51] Hall, *The Hard Road to Renewal*, 47, 49.
[52] Livingstone, 'Monetarism in London', 69.

restore the value of money at the expense of wage labour'.[53] Prynne's thinking in this period foregrounds what he saw as the disaster of Conservative moral economism, as the July 1983 letter to Dorn shows:

> The softness of welfare talk, increasingly discredited, was that both crime and unemployment were produced by social pressures of which in some sense the individual was the hurt victim. The hard line is that in 'reality' there are no victims, so deserving and sponge-like; only those with defective willpower who need the re-educating attrition of the real to compel their self-sufficiency ... once monetarism can be got into the bone marrow of a way of life, the Pay Up or Get Out rule can even be tempered by a little cosmetic philanthropy: foundling hospitals, orphan raffles and the like. We are in for this, and you are, for what I'd guess is close to another decade.[54]

This sinister forecast is constructed from essentially the same critical analysis as Hall's description of Thatcherism's 'translation of a theoretical *ideology* into a populist *idiom*'. *The Oval Window* unfolds and examines this idiom and develops its own brand of poetical *transformism* to do so; its collages are themselves a vantage onto, and a struggle to escape from, the 'new political configuration' that Hall describes.

3 Audible Visions

The Oval Window consists of twenty-seven unnumbered and untitled discrete poems that form a whole sequence. Compared with Prynne's earlier work, the form of *The Oval Window* is most reminiscent of its immediate precursor, *Down Where Changed* (1979), the sequence that Prynne published the year that Thatcher came to power (and the title of which is lifted from the phrase used by *The Times* to describe their stock exchange price listings), though *The Oval Window*'s poems are more varied and expansive than the grim tercets in *Down Where Changed*. Found material from an abundance of sources fills the book from start to finish. Here is the fourth poem of the sequence:

> Coming through with your back turned
> you'd never credit the trick aperture
> in part-supply. Being asked to cut
> into the bone matches wishing to become
> the one that asks and is sharply hurt.
> To be controlled as a matter of urgency:
> don't turn, it's plasma leaking
> > a tune on Monday
> > a renewed drive
> > not doing enough

---

[53] Ibid.   [54] Prynne to Dorn, 17 July 1983.

> to reduce the skin on a grape; the whole
> falling short is wounded vantage in
> talk of the town.[55]

This poem is structured around quotations from two articles in *The Times*,
23 August 1983: 'Health service told to cut more jobs' and 'Managers refuse
to suggest victims', the latter of which concludes a two-part report on the effects
of cuts to the NHS budget, announced on 7 July by the Chancellor of the
Exchequer. 'Coming through with your back turned' deploys the *Times* material
in configuration with an apostrophized or implied subject animated by, and
surrounded with, vocabularies of optical, economic, sadistic, medical, and prosaic significance. This subject is, I suggest, the contested site of Thatcherite
ideology and policy: 'Coming through with your back turned' figures the 'natural
drift towards the private sector' (*The Times*, 22 August 1983, quoting the British
Medical Association's *News Review*), with its attendant destruction of public
welfare, as an economized affective landscape.[56] The first line parodies the
'personal society' and its lauded individualism; it may also be read as
a denunciation of public ignorance of the impetus for, and effects of, cuts to
the NHS indexed by the collage. Indeed, the second-person pronoun ('your
back', 'you'd never credit') mirrors the hated reportage pasted from *The Times*
with a correspondingly gullible and feckless subject. '[Y]ou'd never credit the
trick aperture / in part-supply' frames a false opening onto reality ('trick aperture') in economese ('credit', 'supply'), raising the spectre of a monetarist
fiction. It reads as a metaphorically cramped indication that the apostrophized
subject would not like to believe ('credit') the demonstrably destructive
transformation of the welfare state, in the form of the 'care and facilities' that,
according to *The Times*, were 'certain to suffer'; the subject, after all, is 'Coming
through with [its] back turned'.[57] The whole phrase seems also to refer to the
'part-supply' of daily news stories used to construct the poem, hinting that their
very particularity forms a 'trick aperture' that, ironically, obfuscates the whole-
sale restructuring of the social to which they attest.

   'Being asked to cut / into the bone matches wishing to become / the one that
asks and is sharply hurt' suggests a spurious equivalence ('matches') between the
power indexed by 'cut / into the bone' and the aspirant subject whose wish
to wield such power will see them 'sharply hurt' as a result – 'being asked to
cut into the bone' is lifted from the Bristol health authority's complaint at
government directives to cut costs, as reported in *The Times*.[58] This spurious
equivalence (a figure repeated throughout the sequence, as by the faux-idiomatic

---

[55] *TOW*, 39.   [56] Healy, 'Patient Care and Facilities Certain to Suffer', 4.   [57] Ibid.
[58] Healy, 'Managers Refuse to Suggest Victims', 2.

'Less won't do, / more isn't on either') figures social mobility as movement through a field of lesser or greater exploitation, if such movement wasn't, in any case, simply wishful thinking, rigged, via the verb-to-adverbial mutation from 'cut' to 'sharply', with reflexive violence.[59] '[D]on't turn, it's plasma leaking / a tune on Monday' is a ghoulish symbol of the drained vitality of the health service, and of the social anaemia native to the working week more generally; 'grape[s]' are a foodstuff popularly given to convalescents, so that 'not doing enough / to reduce the skin on a grape' reinforces the image of the cuts as ludicrously punitive. The phrase 'peel me a grape' was made proverbial by Mae West in the 1933 film *I'm No Angel*, in which West's character comically demands of her African American maid that she do so. Given that 'not doing enough to reduce' is lifted from *The Times* ('not doing enough to reduce staff in the health service'), the racial and class divide inscribed, by West's example, into the image of a peeled grape serves to heighten the sense of a preposterous demand placed on the NHS workforce by the country's ruling elite.[60] '[T]he whole / falling short is wounded vantage in / talk of the town' refers back to the 'trick aperture / in part-supply' that 'you'd never credit'. If the 'part-supply' (whether of ideology or reportage) that 'you'd never credit' obscures the very liquidation of the post-war consensus to which Thatcherism aspires, the whole social deficit ('falling short') is nevertheless perceptible only by the 'wounded vantage' that is itself a product of the desperate situation that is everywhere apparent ('talk of the town'). The whole poem – and these last lines in conjunction with their earlier counterparts especially – recalls Prynne's diatribe, in his July 1983 letter to Dorn, against Thatcherism's destabilization 'of the welfare state as an attitude of mind', its desired 're-educating attrition of the real', and its attempt to get monetarism 'into the bone marrow of a way of life'.

The vocabularies that glue the scene of 'Coming through ...' together are deployed, like much of the quoted and non-quoted vocabulary in many of Prynne's sequential poems, in a constellatory manner that accrues significance to individual words systematically, through their relationships between the parts and wholes of individual poems and across the sequence as a whole. The foregoing close reading needs tempering with an indication of the ways in which these vocabularies are picked up and turned over throughout *The Oval Window*, in order to adequately communicate the effects of the poem's

---

[59] *The Times* 25 August issue, which *The Oval Window* quotes in four poems, ran a piece by the technology correspondent Clive Cookson that quotes (the then shadow Home Secretary) Roy Hattersley pointing out that 'Without attempting to organize equality of outcome there can be no social mobility, except for the one in ten thousand individuals of outstanding talent who would rise through the prejudice of the system.' Cookson, 'Hattersley Formula for Equality', 4.

[60] Healy, 'Health Service Told to Cut More Jobs', 1.

compositional method and something of that method's cumulative results. For example, two variations on 'turn' appear in 'Coming through . . .', each of them set in phrasal contexts that are indicative of the everyday horrors of an under-funded NHS, and by metonymic extension, of Thatcherite Britain's assault on the welfare state. Later in the sequence, variations on 'turn' appear set in phrasal contexts redolent with an alternative, far more desirous, even optative signifi-cance. The last lines of the fifteenth poem of the sequence offer a moment of abstract, stylized eroticism that prefigures the amorous, ninth- and tenth-century Chinese lyrics that appear in the later collages of the sequence: 'slowness of gaze / goes down with you, flickering to meet / in both the turn for good'.[61] The twenty-third poem of the sequence includes lines from the second of three concluding songs from Ben Jonson's masque *Love Restored* (1616), lines that in their original context are part of an evocation of the music of the spheres: 'So these did turn, return, advance, / drawn back by doubt, put on by love'.[62] The twenty-seventh and final poem of *The Oval Window* begins with another variation on 'turn', this time in the context of the poem's most explicit expres-sion of subjective longing: 'Standing by the window I heard it, / while waiting for the turn'.[63]

In a poem which proceeds through an enormous amount of recycled material, whether in terms of quoted text or verbal, phrasal, and grammatical mutation, these later variations on 'turn' cannot help but inflect the earlier instances with a proleptic echo of their recollection later in the sequence, whilst the romantic gravity of these later, emphatic usages, is inevitably attenuated by the memory of their earlier evocations of domination. *The Oval Window* is full of these kinds of relationships between verbal, grammatical, phrasal, and tonal parts and wholes. Just as individual poems in the sequence are largely collaged together from newsprint, literary sources, and technical manuals, so the sequence as a whole is most productively read as a dynamic collage of its constituent poems, such that individual words and phrasal units take on the character of a fungible material traded between the poems in a process of reciprocal exchangeability. The semantic value of a word like 'turn' in 'Coming through . . .' is dependent as much upon its capacity to take on the different inflections of its various usages across the whole sequence as it is upon any construable meaning attached to its local appearance. The collage form of *The Oval Window* thus ensures the maintenance of a certain poetical liquidity as the condition of the immediate

---

[61] *TOW*, 50. 'Slowness of gaze' is a quotation from Douglas Oliver's poem 'The Diagonal Is Diagonal', from *The Diagram Poems* (1979). For commentary on Oliver's poem's influence on *The Oval Window*, see Luna, ed., *The Letters of Douglas Oliver and J. H. Prynne, 1967–2000*, xv–xvi.

[62] *TOW*, 59.   [63] Ibid., 63.

value of any of its lexical assets. By the same token, what we might call the textual marketplace of the sequence is itself legible, and its semantic liquidity intelligible, only through the multiple, particular acts of semantic exchange (such as those involved between the different variations on 'turn') that entangle any given poem's individual collage with others in the sequence.

Across the first half of *The Oval Window*, the economized affective landscape of 'Coming through …' segues in and out of the more explicitly financialized interiority of poems such as 'Somewhere else in the market …', in which, as we saw, consciousness (in the form of 'Attention') becomes pegged to stock market fluctuations. Certain poems in the first half of *The Oval Window* describe an historical conjuncture in which political ideology was developing an ever more symbiotic relationship with the empirical priorities and epistemological frameworks of the City of London and its role as a global centre of international capital. The development of this relationship is well attested to in the political and economic histories of the period. Aeron Davis and Catherine Walsh argue that the transformation of the UK economy since the mid-1970s 'was facilitated by a new alliance of financial and emerging state elites against industrial and established state elites'.[64] They point out that the Thatcher governments 'imported personnel … from the financial sector and placed them in charge of the Treasury and Department of Trade and Industry' and that such personnel brought with them 'a very particular financial-market oriented economic philosophy, tools, and disciplinary practices' that provided the 'roadmap' to a more financialized economy.[65] Davis and Walsh identify these practices as follows: 'changes to the tax regime aimed at liberating markets and industries of all kinds', such as the consistent cutting of corporation tax between 1979 and 1989; the privatization policies that 'handed control of large swathes of UK industry directly into the hands of the London Stock Exchange' through flotation (of, for example, whether in part or whole, British Aerospace, Cable and Wireless, and Amersham International between 1981 and 1983, and British Telecom, Rolls-Royce, British Gas, and British Airways between 1983 and 1987), significantly strengthening 'the role of the Exchange as chief allocator of capital in the national economy'; and the legislative programmes (1979–80) that 'brought the release of international exchange and credit controls and initiated a new credit boom', as well as encouraging the 'liberalization of international trade'.[66]

Timo Walter and Leon Wansleben, meanwhile, characterize the period, and the 'new alliance' that Davis and Walsh identify, in far more chaotic and contradictory terms, arguing that 'Thatcherites … failed to bring together

---

[64] Davis and Walsh, 'Distinguishing Financialization from Neoliberalism', 28.   [65] Ibid., 28–9.
[66] Ibid., 41–4.

their anti-inflationary programmatic goals with the technologies of money market management into a durable pragmatic regime' but that successive Conservative governments nevertheless 'unwittingly induced processes of re-alignment between policy techniques and financial market structures that would eventually generate an entirely new macroeconomic governance regime'.[67] Walter and Wansleben further argue that, over the course of the 1980s, 'by reinforcing a process of deindustrialization and accelerated financialization', Thatcher's governments established 'a new context for subsequent attempts to align the new, neoliberal programmes of governing with the market ecologies in which they were to be implemented'.[68] Whilst these histories display a retrospective eloquence and infrastructural overview unavailable to contemporary commentators, the 're-alignment between policy techniques and financial market structures' that engendered new 'market ecologies' is clearly in accord with the contemporary left critique that identified, as Stuart Hall did in 1986, the '*recomposition*' of the British state according to the 'internationalization of capital' and the 'contradictory structure of popular ideology' that Thatcherism so 'effectively exploited . . . playing the discourse of liberal economy and the free market off against the discourse of the organic nation and the disciplined society'.[69] For poets like Prynne, the internal organs of 'popular capitalism' were exposed in every news story about cuts to the NHS or privatization, because such stories spoke to 'Thatcherism's attempt to root its political strategy in the growing fragmentation and individualization [that increasingly characterized] British society'.[70]

Two sections in particular of *The Oval Window* compose a cross-section of this reality:

> A view is a window
> on the real data, not a separate copy
> of that data, or a lower surplus in oil
> and erratic items such as precious stones,
> aircraft and the corpses of men, tigers,
> fish and pythons, "all in a confused tangle."
> Changes to the real data
> are visible through the view; and operations
> against the view are converted, through
> a kind of unofficial window on Treasury policy,
> into operations on the real data.
> To this world given over, now safely,
> work makes free logic joined to the afterlife.[71]   (8)

---

[67] Walter and Wansleben, 'How Central Bankers Learned to Love Financialization', 642.
[68] Ibid.   [69] Hall, *The Hard Road to Renewal*, 85–7.   [70] Ibid., 88.   [71] *TOW*, 43.

> The internal view
> assumes an infinite linear address space,
> a table on which are laid out all
> the rival manuals of self-sufficiency.
> Spring up, O well; sing unto it: but
> the answer is a pool of values in prime
> hock to a pump and its trade-offs.[72]   (10)

Each of these sections is composed largely through collage, the first section (from the eighth poem of the sequence) almost entirely so. C. J. Date's *An Introduction to Database Systems* (1975) provides much of the material, as do *The Times* and *The Financial Times*. In the eighth poem, Date's definition of the term 'view' in database terminology is firstly spliced together with extracts from two newspaper articles: 'Lowest exports this year put Britain in the red' (*The Times*, 25 August 1983) and a report on the centenary of the eruption of Krakatoa. A second quotation from *Database Systems* is then spliced together with a quotation from a report in *The Financial Times* (25 August 1983) about the forecasting work of the National Institute of Economic and Social Research (referred to in the article as 'a kind of unofficial window on Treasury policy'). The line 'into operations on the real data' is Prynne's own, masquerading as his source material. '[W]ork makes free' is a deliberately clunky translation of the German 'Arbeit macht frei', the slogan above the entrances to various Nazi concentration camps, including Auschwitz.

The second section (from the tenth poem of the sequence) collages further quotations from *Database Systems* with Numbers 21:17 ('Spring up, O well; sing ye unto it'), and the term 'trade-offs', that Kerridge and Reeve identify as having been lifted from *The Financial Times* (25 August 1983). In these poems, the technical terminology of database systems suggests a coincidence of external and internal reality – both 'a window / on the real data' and 'The internal view' – in terms of a closed, recursive world of quantifiable information that is the essence of a database. In the eighth poem, 'the real data' is more foundational than other kinds of information, such as the indication of British industrial decline supplied by *The Financial Times* ('lower surplus in oil') or the 'corpses of men' and other organic detritus thrown into the ocean by the eruption of Krakatoa – these compose a metaphor for the messily incalculable nature of human life in general ('all in a confused tangle').[73] That 'operations / against the

---

[72] Ibid., 45.

[73] Reeve and Kerridge quote the source of 'all in a confused tangle' as an unidentified newspaper article preserved in Prynne's archive (*TOW*, 103). The phrase is also reminiscent of Pound's translation of Li Po's 'Exile's Letter': 'It is like the flowers falling at Spring's end / Confused, whirled in a tangle'. See Pound, *Translations*, 197. My thanks to the anonymous reviewer who pointed out this connection.

view are converted / though a kind of unofficial window on Treasury policy, / into operations on the real data' suggests a relationship to the 'real' mediated by the organs of proto-governance that forecast the likely outcomes and effects of the economy; in the article from which Prynne adapted the lines beginning 'a lower surplus in oil', this forecast is 'gloomy'.[74] These lines thus collage an image of economic performativity, in the sense suggested by the economic sociologist Michel Callon, and developed by Donald MacKenzie in his theory of financial economics, especially of options pricing models since the 1970s: that such economics 'performs, shapes and formats the economy' rather than passively reflecting it, especially those models and formulae incorporated into the 'algorithms, routines, and procedures' of financial behaviour.[75]

'To this world given over, now safely' appeals, by a pun on the so-called givens or givenness of experience, to the 'world' of baked-in futurity heavily implied by the jargon of database systems and the epistemologies of economic/ financial prophecy alike. The line summarizes the recursive temporal logic of financialized capital, for which (*pace* Joseph Vogl) 'future expectations can be translated into expected futures', ensuring that, 'in the long run, homogeneity between the future present and the present future is more or less guaranteed to prevail'.[76] The safety that this engenders ('now safely') is capital's own, hence the final line's invocation of the Nazi acceleration of capital's inhuman 'logic' to the point of genocidal conversion of life into 'the afterlife'. This last couplet is also a dry, Frankfurt School–style joke about the everyday fascism that inheres in populist authoritarianism and its hatred of the unemployed. The tenth poem of the sequence is the subjective correlate to the 'view' on the 'real data' of the eighth: it composes a collage of similar materials to the tenth (Date's *Database Systems*, *Financial Times* reportage) from the perspective of 'The internal view'. The pun on 'table' produces an image of interiority as a vast data set, as infinitely self-referential as 'the world given over' produced in the eighth poem. From 'Spring up' to 'trade-offs', the poem composes a recursive image of domination familiar from the ideological hall of mirrors in 'Coming through with your back turned', though here the image is more explicitly yoked to Thatcherite individualization by 'the rival manuals of self-sufficiency' that characterize the ideological 'address space' of the individual. 'Spring up, O well; sing unto it: but / the answer is a pool of values in prime / hock to a pump and its trade-offs': these lines collage into a dialogic exchange what is essentially a scriptural work song, sung as the Israelites dig a well in the wilderness, with an 'answer' that subordinates the products of that labour

---

[74] Wilson-Smith, 'Lowest Exports This Year Put Britain in the Red', 1.

[75] MacKenzie, *An Engine, Not a Camera*, 16, 19.   [76] Vogl, *The Specter of Capital*, 78.

('pool' and 'pump' both suggest drawing water from a well) to the nested set of financial euphemisms – and thus to a realm of fungible, indiscriminate abstraction – into which they are embedded. The eighth and tenth poems' images of a hatefully self-replicating reality are summarized by *The Oval Window*'s most fulsomely dejected lines a couple of poems later, in the twelfth poem's laconic opening clarification: 'So what you do is enslaved non-stop / to perdition of sense by leakage / into the cycle'.[77]

These sections from *The Oval Window* represent Prynne's most developed evocation of financialized life before *Bands around the Throat*. They evoke such life as part of *The Oval Window*'s examination of the ideological and political priorities of Thatcherism in the first half of the poem, and their unfolding of a financialized subjectivity is subordinated to those priorities and to the poem's venomous attitude towards its political context. In *Bands around the Throat*, the compositional priorities of the poems become more fully embedded within the world of financial imperatives, epistemologies, and actors, at an historical moment, post–Big Bang, in which these imperatives, epistemologies, and actors rise to prominence on the stage of global capital. I turn to these poems shortly in order to trace the development of Prynne's writing through the 1980s. Before doing so, I want to reflect on the ways in which *The Oval Window*'s second half maintains the poem's commitment to its collage method, whilst drastically altering the preponderance of collaged materials from newspaper clippings (though these still appear) to ninth- and tenth-century Chinese *tz'u* lyrics, translated by Lois Fusek, which Prynne read in Fusek's edition of the *Hua-chien chi*, *Among the Flowers* (1982). *The Oval Window* seems to shift drastically in its second half (from the eighteenth to the twenty-sixth poems) from being a sequence about Thatcherism to being a sequence 'about' moonlight, snow, and pear blossom, through which is laced, nevertheless, lines and vocabularies which refer back to a system in thrall to the 'relative cyclical downturn[s]' of an increasingly financialized economy and its ideological imperatives. Why does this happen?

Chinese *tz'u* lyrics are a highly stylized form of 'verbal notation' for songs originally set to music, composed by court poets on erotic themes. The 'world depicted in *Among the Flowers* is the world of the courtesan and the singing-girl, the beautiful "flowers"' of the anthology's title.[78] As Kerridge points out, the lyrics' original context of composition, 'during and after the collapse of the T'ang dynasty … was a time of war and widespread social breakdown, but these highly conventional lyrics mostly adopt familiar love-story scenarios' and 'formulaic' environmental vistas: 'what they can mean is severely restricted and

---

[77] *TOW*, 110.   [78] Fusek, *Among the Flowers*, 3, 1.

entirely predetermined by the traditional code that they invoke'.[79] The seventeenth poem of *The Oval Window* ('At the onset of the single life') introduces a series of references to the eponymous 'oval window' that recur throughout the second half of the sequence. The phrase derives, as Kerridge and Reeve explain, from the name for the 'aperture in the middle ear through which sound waves pass to be converted into neural impulses'.[80] In the poem, the term is accorded something of the inter-contextual fungibility that characterizes other significant vocabularies, and its usages across the second half of the sequence encompass sensory associations apart from hearing (taste and sight, for example), but these associations orbit, and finally come to rest (in the final poem of the sequence), in the auditory symbolism generated from the term's anatomical meaning ('Standing by the window I heard it').[81] In most of the poems in which 'the oval window' (or simply 'the window') appears in the second half of the sequence, it is collaged into close proximity with material from the *tz'u* lyrics, along with references to the politics and economy of the United Kingdom that so dominate the poems earlier in the sequence.

To give a sense of these later poems, here is the nineteenth:

> Her wrists shine white like the frosted snow;
> they call each other to the south stream.
> The oval window is closed in life,
> by the foot-piece of the stapes. Chill shadows
> fall from the topmost eaves, clear waters
> run beside the blossoming peach. Inside
> this window is the perilymph of the vestibule.
>   Now O now I needs must part,
>   parting though I absent mourne.
> It is a child's toy, shaken back in
> myopic eddies by the slanting bridge:
> toxic; dangerous fire risk; bright moonlight
> floods the steps like a cascade of water.[82]

From 'Her wrists ...' to 'I absent mourne' the poem is entirely collaged together. The first two lines each derive from a different *tz'u* lyric; their combined effect is that 'Her wrists' take on a life of their own and 'call each other to the south stream', an act of figurative dismemberment that ruptures the coherence of the *tz'u* whilst creating an original grammatical coherence. This technique is repeated often in the deployment of the *tz'u* lyrics: their codified, aesthetic referential matrix of snow, moonlight, and courtesan is both disturbed and made contiguous with the setting of the collage. 'The oval window is

---

[79] *TOW*, 27–8.   [80] Reeve and Kerridge, *Nearly Too Much*, 152.   [81] *TOW*, 63.
[82] *TOW*, 55.

closed in life, / by the foot-piece of the stapes' and 'Inside / this window is the perilymph of the vestibule' are taken from a surgical textbook, *Last's Anatomy*. 'Chill shadows ...' to 'blossoming peach' splice together two *tz'u* lyrics. 'Now O now ...' quotes Dowland's song of the same name. The two lines of inset Elizabethan lute song mimic the thematic concern with parting lovers that is a staple of the *tz'u* lyrics; their inclusion suggests a specific, though arbitrary, aesthetic parity between the English and Chinese traditions, despite their historical, linguistic, and cultural differences.[83] '[B]y the slanting bridge' and 'bright moonlight / floods the steps like a cascade of water' quote more *tz'u* lyrics. Prynne's only original lines in the poem are 'It is a child's toy, shaken back in / myopic eddies' and 'toxic; dangerous fire risk'. The first lines refer to an object repeatedly invoked across the second half of the sequence, 'a toy with a snowstorm' (18).[84] This object is referred to, with diminishing affection but rising feeling, as 'A child's joy' (18), a 'child's toy' (19), a 'childish' toy (26), and a 'toy hard to bear' (27).[85] Its miniature, snowy diorama suggests both the world of the *tz'u* lyrics and the perceptual facility of the inner ear. The object gathers and triangulates all three (ear, *tz'u*, toy) by metonymic association with the 'tiny calcite crystals' of the inner ear that 'resemble snowflakes' under the microscope, and which are 'responsible for providing the brain with information as to the position of the head within the earth's gravitational field'.[86] That the 'toy' is 'shaken back in / myopic eddies' thus insinuates both a childish (though no less real) pleasure in aesthetic obfuscation and an accompanying perceptual/intellectual disorientation. Even in these 'original' lines, however, there is a legible literary inheritance in the use, and contextual development throughout the rest of the sequence, of the word 'toy'. Kerridge points out the influence of Coleridge's 'Frost at Midnight' ('the idling Spirit' that, 'every where / Echo or mirror seeking of itself, / makes a toy of Thought') on what he calls a 'combination of expansive and diminutive pressure around the word "toy"' in Prynne's poem.[87]

---

[83] Prynne has since remarked on the mutual venerability of the English and Chinese poetic traditions; see 'Keynote Speech at the First Pearl River Poetry Conference'. Of particular relevance is Prynne's assertion in this speech that '[e]very poet requires his daily dose of natural language to replenish his storehouse of sweetness and horrors. And so the press and the TV and all the rest of the normal practice of degraded and corrupted language are absolutely essential to poets, and they're particularly so because they give poets the task and the duty of knowing where they are and knowing what they do' (12).

[84] *TOW*, 54.

[85] Ibid., 54–5, 62–3. The affective progress of these descriptions, from simple pleasure to rueful forbearance, is indexical of the second half of the sequence's progress through fantasy to disillusionment, which I detail in this section.

[86] Reeve and Kerridge, *Nearly Too Much*, 152–3.   [87] *TOW*, 26.

To read the second half of *The Oval Window* according to the design of its collage is to recognize a distinct shift in the materials arranged, from those which document the rubbish interior of a privatized subject and its 'infinite linear address space' to those that juxtapose the physiology of audibility and orientation with an ancient form of poetic song.[88] It is to recognize, furthermore, a shift in the attentions of the collage from a distinctly (though not exclusively) British political and economic referential field to an equally distinctive internationalist purview, through which national, historical, and even legal borders are symbolically, and, in the case of copyright law, literally contravened by the collaged materials. Prynne, after all, takes Lois Fusek's translations of the *tz'u* lyrics and puts them in his own poem, not a year after their original publication.[89] In the nineteenth poem, 'the oval window', 'closed in life', is surrounded by *tz'u* material that is itself a 'verbal notation' signifying a historical relation to popular song. In moments such as this – which become increasingly strained almost as soon as they are introduced – the collage indulges in a synaesthetic, auditory vision, or a vision of audibility, that temporarily floods the very fungibility of its verbal architecture, its lexical liquidity, with the richly intercalated metonymy of ear/*tz'u*/toy.[90] Another of these moments occurs in the twenty-second poem (the italicized words are *tz'u* lyrics): '*A light wind crosses the fragrant waters*; / deaf to reason I cup my hands, to / *dew-drenched apricot flowers* and their / livid tranquillity'.[91] The authorial figure, 'deaf to reason', like a child having a tantrum, but surrounded in the collage by fragments (and the fragrance) of elegant song, performs a gesture of entreaty to the 'livid tranquillity' of the *tz'u* lyrics' unheard melodies. Thus, a poetical transformism trained in the early poems of the sequence on the ideologically programmable subject of populist authoritarianism, a codified humanity, whose 'Attention is low in historic terms', is flooded, between the eighteenth and twenty-sixth poems, with the historical fragments of an extremely human code, snapshots of an artifice at once impersonal, elite,

---

[88] *TOW*, 48, 45.

[89] Prynne sent Fusek a copy of *The Oval Window* and his review, in *Modern Asian Studies*, of *New Songs from a Jade Terrace: An Anthology of Early Chinese Love Poetry* (translated by Anne Birrell) on 10 December 1983, writing: 'I hope you will not mind the latterday instances of *huan-ku* and *tuo-t'ai*: I read your version of the *Hua-chien chi* with much interest & admiration.' The 'instances of *huan-ku* and *tuo-t'ai*' (literally 'changing the bones' and 'escaping the embryo') refer to Prynne's borrowings; these alchemical terms were used by the Northern Sung Dynasty poet Huang T'ing-chien to describe his 'creative imitation' of earlier poets. See Nienhauser, ed., *The Indiana Companion to Traditional Chinese Literature*, 447. Fusek replied on 12 June 1984, thanking Prynne for the book and review and writing that 'I was enormously interested and intrigued by the ways in which you were using lines here and there from the *tz'u* in the *Hua-chien chi*, and by the sure sense of language in the poems themselves'. Prynne to Fusek, 10 December 1983; Fusek to Prynne, 12 June 1984. J. H. Prynne Papers.

[90] Fusek, *Among the Flowers*, 3.   [91] *TOW*, 58.

aristocratic, and beautiful. The 'world given over' is inversely matched by
a dream of the self given over to, or dispersed amongst, its objects of aesthetic
contemplation, a process laced with the Coleridgean pathos of the 'idling Spirit'
and its play of thought.

This vision is, in itself, unconstrained by its inaccessibility 'in life', though
the figurative dismemberment and self-conscious reanimation of the *tz'u* lyrics
(so that, for example, 'Her wrists ... call each other') ensure that it hardly
presents as utopian; the *tz'u* are either broken in half or made to share
a grammatical and/or syntactical continuity with the imperatives of, for
example, the Department for Health and Social Services, as in the twenty-
second poem. The vision's unsustainability is immediately recognized in the
nineteenth poem not just by the unstable ambivalence of the designation 'It is
a child's toy' but also by the second line of authorial 'intervention' in the poem's
collage, 'toxic; dangerous fire risk', as if the combinatorial intensity of the
surrounding material and the vision it maintains were liable to burn up on closer
inspection. Which indeed they do, as in the twenty-third poem 'there is burning
along / this frame', and in the twenty-fourth poem what is by now quite self-
evidently a fantasy of acute chinoiserie becomes prey to the historical, political,
and ideological contexts that are so preciously avoided in the original *tz'u*.[92]
The lines in the twenty-fourth poem 'Not feudal / nor slave-owning but the
asiatic [*sic*] mode / as locally communal within a despotic state: / the slant of
imperium coming sideways' anticipate the consolidation of the war-torn Five
Dynasties under the sovereignty of the Sung Dynasty, as well as flag up the
delusion of artistic autonomy required to ring-fence a vision of aesthetic
'tranquillity' in the face of any 'despotic state', whether in tenth-century
China or twentieth-century England.[93] By the twenty-sixth poem, the fragments
of *tz'u* lyrics have become helpless figments, brittle enough to snap into
a merely metaphorical irony: 'These *petals, crimson and pink*, / are cheque
stubs, spilling chalk in a *mist /of soft azure*'.[94] This penultimate poem also refers
back to the political imperatives of privatization and to the disintegration of the
welfare state: the lines 'At the last we want / unit costs plus VAT, patient
grading: / made to order, made to care' are a bitter caricature of the market
logic of private healthcare, by the lights of which the 'patient' is afforded a place

---

[92] Ibid., 59–60.
[93] Ibid., 60. For an extensive treatment of *The Oval Window*'s later poems' 'concerns about the
political history of China through to the immediate post-Maoist era', and of the 'textual history'
they invoke that 'plays with the idea of capital as a kind of circulation of memory-states', see
Dobran, 'The Difficult Style', 268–73.
[94] *TOW*, 62.

in the queue by their ability to offset their own 'unit costs' and 'care' is a commodity 'made to order'.[95]

The last lines of *The Oval Window*'s final poem recall the last lines of its first poem:

> What can't be helped
> is the vantage, private and inert; yet
> in a twinkling mind you, to pick up
> elastic replacements on the bench code.[96]　　　　　　　　　(1)

> Beyond help it is a joy at death itself:
> a toy hard to bear, laughing all night.[97]　　　　　　　　　(27)

The last lines of the first poem are a miniature, summative overture of the entire sequence. The 'vantage, private and inert' introduces the *prospectus* of, and for, a subjectivity that, in subsequent poems of the sequence, is colonized by the terms of Thatcherite individualization, prominent amongst which are the political imperatives of privatization. The next lines foreshadow the seductive attraction and the unreality of the auditory vision afforded by the ear/*tz'u*/toy matrix in the second half of the sequence. They do so by assembling their suggestion of a miraculous transformation from three distinct elements: the language of Paul's promise to the Corinthians of the life everlasting ('In a moment, in the twinkling of an eye ... the dead shall be raised incorruptible', Corinthians 15:51–52), lines that infer the purchase of superficial alternatives to 'the vantage' ('to pick up / elastic replacements') and the language of programmable virtuality: bench coding is 'the construction of virtual environments in which software is tested'.[98] The last lines of the twenty-seventh poem return to the 'vantage' that 'can't be helped' and to its abnegation of life for 'joy at death itself' that recalls the fascistic overtones of authoritarian populism invoked in the eighth poem. The implied vantage, by now enriched with all the associations of political subjectivity which render it 'Beyond help', is finally enjambed into identification with the 'toy hard to bear', and hence into association with the unsustainable fantasy unfolded through the ear/*tz'u*/toy metonymy. Both vision and reality are trapped in the same cycle. The vision contradicts the dismal reality of British parliamentary democracy, in the shape of an exquisite, autonomous artifice populated by the pseudo-imperial vistas of tenth-century China, its images and sounds 'made to order', the courtesans 'made to care', and the whole artifice assembled according to the ancient instructions of its aesthetic code. The fantasy does not collapse because of the gender dynamics which

---

[95] Ibid.　　[96] Ibid., 36.　　[97] Ibid., 63.　　[98] Ibid., 23.

inhere in the *tz'u* tradition and the world of indentured prostitution which they romanticize. It collapses because it is a fantasy, a dream of retrenchment from the economized and financialized self of the 'personal society', and into what is, as Ryan Dobran argues, 'an illusory and discomforting foil'.[99]

What the vision portends is, however, of eminently less value than what the poem achieves through its collage method. What this method models – not just in the *tz'u*-suffused poems but throughout – has two distinct but related facets. The poem collates and arranges its sources of information about the world: it manages this information through a verbal and phrasal liquidity which determines its field of reference and its shades of meaning, from scornful despair to 'livid tranquillity' and back again. In this regard, *The Oval Window* reflects an emerging financialized reality for which the data of economic activity are the material out of which 'this world given over' and our own horizons and possibilities of meaning are composed and reproduced. But what lends the compositional logic of *The Oval Window* such an infrastructure of ventriloquized domination is also that which enables the indissoluble differences that characterize its collaged objects to be legible *as* differences – not just in the annotated edition but in the very way the poem is put together that the annotated edition makes plain. The collage method developed in *The Oval Window* displays in sequential unity the objects coerced into its world picture, but it is the shimmering tension between these objects and their vocabularies and registers of meaning, as they flit back and forth across its twenty-seven screens, that makes *The Oval Window* mean something in excess of the world merely 'given over' to its endless reproduction, to what one of its resonant, inset quotations from a programming manual calls the 'solution … defined in terms of itself'.[100] Prynne's collage proceeds through incessant recomposition to maintain the heterogeneity of its objects, in the same breath as it composes a window onto a world built according to the 'rival manuals of self-sufficiency'.[101] And in this sense, through its very systematicity, *The Oval Window* begins to dramatize a kind of heterotopic anti-system of knowledge. This knowledge is irreducible to the archive of fact and opinion about policy and legislation in *The Times*, or to the data processed by the Institute for Economic and Social Research, the Department for Health and Social Services, or the financial markets, because it is an inherently relational and processual

---

[99] Dobran, 'The Difficult Style', 274. It is difficult not to hear in *The Oval Window*'s doomed Chinese escape route a meta-commentary on the entire career, but also the particular literary and cultural obsessions, of Pound. Pound, of course, prized (often mistaken translations of) Chinese literature, and the treatment of the *tz'u* lyrics in *The Oval Window* might even be said to constitute something of an ironic eulogy for Pound's own passionate, but equally doomed (in the sense of being entrained into the *Cantos*' finally incoherent sprawl) appropriation of Chinese literature.
[100] *TOW*, 47.   [101] Ibid., 45.

knowledge, as physiological as it is intellectual, and as much heard, seen, and felt as it is known. Not all poems in *The Oval Window* evince the heterotopic possibilities of its collage method equally, or equally successfully. Some, like 'Somewhere else in the market . . .', are so stuffed with the depressing register of newsprint that they fail to evince much beyond a wry grimace at a blankly unavoidable reality: the 'shockwave of basic revulsion' that Prynne describes in his July 1983 letter to Dorn.[102] But even in these early poems of the sequence, the collage develops a modus operandi that contributes to its uneven anti-systematicity, and to its polyvalent *prospectus* of human life in the midst of its systemic calculation.

4 Strangled Songs

In many ways, *Bands around the Throat* is a far less ambitious collection than *The Oval Window*. None of its fourteen, discrete, titled poems are capacious enough to develop anything like *The Oval Window*'s serial complexity. By comparison with the comprehensive anti-systematicity of *The Oval Window*, the poems collected in *Bands around the Throat* are a far more occasional set of verses. Much like the contemporary work of Barry MacSweeney, Anna Mendelssohn, Douglas Oliver, and Tom Raworth, the poems in *Bands around the Throat* dramatize, lament, and contest Thatcherite ideological, economic, and political power. Written between 1985 and 1987 and published in direct anticipation of Thatcher's re-election in June 1987, the collection eschews the constellatory development of *The Oval Window* in favour of much shorter and even more condensed collages, the referential fields of which nevertheless share some important objects, language features, and themes. Chief amongst these are quotation from, reference to, and subject matter gleaned from newsprint. Most of the poems collected in *Bands around the Throat* share with each other a deep structural reliance on *The Times*, upon which they draw for inspiration and metaphorical coherence as much as for source material in terms of quotation, part-quotation, and adapted-quotation. This reliance on *The Times* underpins the poems' relationship to the world to a greater extent than the poems in *The Oval Window*. In the earlier sequence, newsprint supplies the ongoing evidence of political and economic recomposition in the United Kingdom. Newsprint in *The Oval Window* is also indexical of a reality which the poem attempts to diagnose and imagine a way out of, with the result that this imagination and its virtual, 'elastic replacements' become subject to the same diagnosis of programmed overdetermination which conditions the 'vantage, private and inert' in the first place. Only through the internally contradictory arrangement of its collaged

---

[102] Prynne to Dorn, 17 July 1983.

parts does *The Oval Window* evince a fragile, near fugitive sense of heterogen-
ous syncretism beyond the 'self-sufficiency' of the political and economic
whole it depicts. In *Bands around the Throat*, newsprint continues to provide
a material base of reportage about Thatcherism, mediated by the establishment-
arian, pro-Tory editorial practice of *The Times*. But in poems such as 'Fool's
Bracelet', 'Almost Lunch-Time', 'In the Pink', and 'Rates of Return', the
stories quoted or adapted from *The Times* also tell a bigger story about changes
to the relationships between information technologies, global financial markets,
and political power that illuminates both national policy and international trends
in finance.

Prynne followed these developments through his reading (both in *The Times*
and in the wider literature) and referred to them in his correspondence.
A postcard sent to the Dorns on 14 October 1986 reads in part: 'At home we
got a hastening switch to a screen market, and in the viewfinder a blank, worn
out dismay. Dare we affirm, we been here before, in the same bin? Too Right:
Big Bang: Not Many Dead (yet): J.'[103] The tone of this note is familiar from the
letters to the Dorns cited in Section 2: it is wryly despairing, matching the pace
of newsworthy developments with its own quick-witted gallows humour.[104]
The 'hastening switch to a screen market' refers to the widely publicized
introduction of the electronic marketplace, Stock Exchange Automated
Quotations (SEAQ), as part of the roll-out of legal, technical, and infrastructural
reforms to the UK financial sector that occurred on 27 October 1986, an event
known in financial history as 'Big Bang'. SEAQ, 'initially code-named
SEMANTIC (for Stock Exchange Market ANd Trade Information Computer)',
was developed in order to capitalize on the reorganization of the London Stock
Exchange according to the precepts of greater competition, streamlined effi-
ciency, and the internationalization of London's financial markets.[105] Big Bang,
as one history of the London Stock Exchange recounts, transformed

> the structure and organisation of the London Stock Exchange as well as . . .
> the physical market it provided. Membership was extended to any who
> wished to join, including banks and foreign brokers who had previously
> been excluded . . . The buying and selling of securities was no longer confined
> to the trading floor located in the London Stock Exchange but could take
> place through office-to-office telephone links based on current prices dis-
> played on computer screens.[106]

---

[103] Prynne to Dorn, 14 October 1986. J. H. Prynne Papers.
[104] The play with 'been'/'bin' refers to an old, punning joke between Prynne and Dorn, based on the
fact that 'the British "been" sounds like the American "bean", and the American "been" sounds
like the British "bin"'. See Katko, 'Relativistic Phytosophy', 256n41.
[105] Pardo-Guerra, *Automating Finance*, 141.
[106] Bellringer and Michie, 'Big Bang in the City of London', 117.

In the years leading up to the changes, *The Times* reported on the anticipation and anxiety surrounding Big Bang from political and City sources, and in the weeks and months following 27 October 1986, on the effects that Big Bang produced. The newspaper also often carried advertisements by securities houses, banks, and financial services companies declaring the epochal importance of the changes and the necessity of preparing for and adapting to them. On the day Prynne sent his postcard to the Dorns, for example, *The Times* carried a half-page advertisement for the stockbrokers Phillips & Drew, which declared 'AFTER THE BIG BANG, THE SURVIVAL OF THE FITTEST', and presented its claims about the 'next stage in the Development of the Species' etched into a graphic of a stone tablet, insinuating that Big Bang was both part of an evolutionary necessity stretching from the origins of the universe to the present day and a revelation handed down to mankind from on high.[107]

Whilst the market neither autonomously evolved on its own terms nor changed on 27 October in ways that can solely be ascribed to the abolition of fixed commissions and so-called single capacity (the strict division between stockjobbers and stockbrokers) that were the objects of government-induced reform, Phillips & Drew's bizarre yoking together of competing orders of historical significance captures something of the complex motivations for, and outcomes of, Big Bang. And whilst an exact causation between the City interests absorbed into the successive Thatcher governments of the 1980s and the specific effects of Big Bang is difficult to establish with any certainty, contemporary accounts and retrospective histories agree that 'policy was driven by the desire [in government] to restore the UK's financial sector to a central position in the global economic system by making London more open and competitive', replicating at the level of financial (de)regulation the logic of unfettered free-market competition that underpinned privatization drives in the health system. City technologists, meanwhile, inspired by the New York Stock Exchange's NASDAQ system, leapt at the 'pivotal opportunity . . . to reengineer the marketplace and its organisation' and to 'build the market anew, atop a single and elegant infrastructure' that would liberate the market, and the market makers, from the inefficient physicality of the Stock Exchange floor itself.[108] The infrastructure that came to fruition on 27 October, however, was not quite as 'elegant' as some had hoped. It was instead, argues the period's most technology-focussed historian, 'a product of creative recombinant bricolage', built around SEAQ's ability to centralize the Exchange's existing, legacy technologies through the 'crucial organizational innovation' of its custom-built terminal display system: '[l]inking communications through phones and

---

[107] *The Times*, 14 October 1986, 22.   [108] Pardo-Guerra, *Automating Finance*, 136–7.

representations through real-time price reporting and visualization systems, SEAQ made an electronic market actionable with technological means.'[109]

On the day of Big Bang, *The Times* devoted a full page to explaining SEAQ's provenance, necessity, and the arrangement and meaning of its display screen (including an annotated screenshot), under the headline 'The technology that had to come':

> Although the trading floor will continue after October 27, there will in theory be no need for broker/dealers and market makers (the two main categories of players after Big Bang) to visit the Stock Exchange. All they will need is SEAQ, to provide information on bid and offer prices and trades, and a telephone to call another trader to execute the deal. In time, dealers will be able to use SEAQ to execute some of their trades.[110]

SEAQ is one instance of the revolution in technologies of capital flows that transformed the world's major exchanges in the 1970s and 1980s. Its screen-based appresentation of the market 'through real-time price reporting and visualization' makes it an example of what has since been called a 'scopic' medium of market coordination, a 'system of observation and projection that assembles on one surface dispersed and diverse activities, interpretations and representations which in turn orient and constrain the response of an audience'.[111] This 'surface' is the screen itself: the reflected reality of a globally integrated information system. The development of London's screen market, therefore, partakes of a new kind of knowledge management native to the ascendency of financialized capital, in the form of flows of news and price information that SEAQ, and the legacy systems that it centralized and coordinated, collated and projected on the trader's screen/s. Both the material ramifications and the spirit of these developments, I suggest, directly influence the form and content of Prynne's collages in *Bands around the Throat*. The discrete, titled poems therein are, like SEAQ, 'quote driven system[s]' – they present a dizzying array of textual source material that coordinates and projects a world, in the form of a selection of possible literary, textual, and informational relationships to, or allegories for, that world, but a selection the total meaning of which is irreducible to any one of these relationships.[112] The poems are assemblages that mimic the form of information

[109] Ibid., 139, 143, 145.   [110] Lander, 'The Technology That Had to Come', 31.

[111] Pardo-Guerra, *Automating Finance*, 145; Cetina and Preda, 'The Temporalization of Financial Markets', 126. I follow Cetina and Preda's adaptation of the Husserlian term 'appresentation' – which Husserl uses in his phenomenology to indicate the '*making "co-present"*' of objects, including other people, for consciousness – to refer to the way in which the screen market 'deliver[s] not only transnational situations, but a global world spanning all major time zones' for traders who 'simultaneously confront the market and [are] part of it'. See Husserl, *Cartesian Meditations*, 109; Cetina and Preda, 'The Temporalization of Financial Markets', 127.

[112] Lander, 'The Technology That Had to Come', 31.

replicated on the SEAQ screens: representations of a self-referential totality, or a closed system, a system which nevertheless 'present[s] layers of context and horizons' that inform the transactional nature of the system and feed its network of possible meanings.[113] The poems are mimetic to the extent that they imitate the formal and visual logic of the screen market. But they make this logic appear out of the philological network of textual interconnection of which the poems are composed; their mimesis is therefore an imitation of that which cannot appear appresentationally; it is a mimesis of the historical depth of the ideological frameworks that remain subservient to appearance itself.

The first poem in *Bands around the Throat* has a special connection to the context just sketched, because it thematizes share selling and buying (and does so by reflecting a scene of financial trading made possible by the technology discussed in this section), satirizes the financialization of the citizen-subject through a literary-dramatic beheading (punning on the 'execution' of a trade in the process), and locates these (and its other) objects in relation to the anticipated re-election of Thatcher on 11 June 1987. Here is the poem in full, its sources annotated for reference.[114]

Fool's Bracelet[115]

In the day park shared by advancement
the waiting clients make room, for another
rising bunch of lifetime disposals.[116] It is

---

[113] Cetina, 'From Pipes to Scopes', 8.

[114] The sources identified in the annotations (and those provided for 'Almost Lunch-Time' in this section) draw on materials preserved in Prynne's archive where noted but are otherwise drawn from the *Times Digital Archive* and Google.

[115] Prynne, *Poems*, 342. See the transcription of the Revesby Play in Chambers, *The English Folk-Play*, 112: 'Our old Fool's bracelet is not made of gold, / But it is made of iron and good steel, / And unto death we'll make this old fool yield.' A hand-written bibliography for the folk play sources for 'Fool's Bracelet' is preserved in Prynne's archive. It includes the studies by Brody, Cawte et al., Chambers, and Helm cited in the Notes, as well as articles by Helm and R. J. E. Tiddy's *The Mummers' Play* (1923). See also Phillips, 'The Sound of Money', 14, quoting Bob Beckman: 'The market is rising because of "The Greater Fool Theory". You buy a share in . . . the hope that a greater fool will eventually pay more for it. In the end it is bought by the "Greatest Fool of All", just before the end.'

[116] See Phillips, 'Taking Stocks to Stores', 12: 'Privatization has spread share buying across the population and the across the land . . . It has meant that [John Cox, the manager of the Bristol branch of Quilter Goodison's Money Centre] has had to deploy a few shopkeeper's skills that stockbroking does not normally require, like judging when is the right time to approach a hovering client with a "Can I help you, sir?"' The article's accompanying photograph depicts the Quilter Goodison Company (QGC) Money Centre in Debenhams, Bristol, featuring a number of waiting clients. For 'rising', see Note 115 ('The market is rising'). For 'lifetime', see 'Liffe [London International Financial Futures Exchange] trading almost doubled last year', *The Times*, 12 May 1987, 21. For 'disposals', see 'Wilting Lilley Aims for Revival', *The Times*, 12 May 1987, 20: 'Disposals in North America could be the next plan of the new management team, though a more pressing problem is an overall capital restructure.' Whilst these terms are

the next round in the sing-song by treble touches,
a high start not detained by the option   5
of a dream to pass right on through[117]
the spirit proof coming off the top.[118] What
don't you want, is there no true end
to grief at joy, casting away deterrent hope[119]
in a spate of root filling? The upside of the song[120]   10
from the valley below[121] excites lock-tremors[122]

---

obviously not confined to *The Times*, I cite their usage in the 12 May edition (and that of 'spate',
'upside', 'proxy', and 'flotation', Notes 120, 123, and 136) in order to emphasize the influence
of this issue on the poem as a whole.

[117] See Clark, 'Election Date Lifts Shares to Two-Day Gain of £15bn', 20: 'Dealers described it
[the £7 billion added to the value of quoted shares the previous day] as a "dream start" to the
new, three-week account as prices raced away from the beginning in anticipation of the Prime
Minister's announcements.'

[118] See Tate and Smith, 'Shares Peak on Poll News', 19: 'Stock market dealers are convinced that
a Thatcher Government will be returned for a third time, which will lead to a huge influx of
overseas investment money into the UK. Their optimism was further fueled by talk of a further
imminent cut in bank base rates. Ironically, share prices started to come off the top only minutes
before Mrs Thatcher's announcement of the election.'

[119] See Yeats, *The Countess Cathleen*: 'Some sell because the money gleams, and some / Because
they are in terror of the grave, / And some because their neighbours sold before, / And some
because there is a kind of joy / In casting hope away, in losing joy, / In ceasing all resistance, in at
last / Opening one's arms to the eternal flames, / In casting all sails out upon the wind; / To this—
full of the gaity of the lost—/ Would all folk hurry if your gold were gone.' *The Collected Plays
of W. B. Yeats*, 31. *The Countess Cathleen* is widely considered neo-medieval in form and recalls
the tradition of mystery/miracle and morality plays. Prynne was almost certainly put in mind of
Yeats's connection to the morality play by Robert Potter's discussion of Yeats's *The Hour Glass*
in *The English Morality Play*, 228–31. Photocopies of the title page, colophon, and page 249 of
Potter's book are preserved in Prynne's archive (see Note 131).

[120] For 'spate', see Clark, 'Election Date Lifts Shares to Two-Day Gain of £15bn', 20: 'Ladbroke, the
betting, property and leisure group, continued to rally after the spate of rumours which have hit the
shares in recent weeks, climbing by 10p to 417p as more than 7 million shares changed hands.' For
'upside', see Fleet, 'The Bank of England Takes a Neutral Stance', 21: 'Thus, the upside for sterling
against the mark is limited, and exchange rates may have already begun to adjust to this possibility.'

[121] See 'Early One Morning' (Roud no. 12682): 'Early one morning, just as the sun was rising,
I heard a maid sing in the valley below.' There are many versions; Chappell prints this opening
of the song beneath the tune. See Chappell, *Popular Music of the Olden Time*, 735–6.

[122] For 'lock', see Chambers, *The English Folk-Play*, 107: '*They all re-enter, and lock their swords
to make the glass, The Fool running about the room*'. Chambers explains:

> There is a persistent figure [in the Sword Dance], sometimes occurring more than once
> in the course of a dance, in which each dancer presses the hilt of his sword under the
> point of his neighbour's, so as to mesh the swords together tightly and securely in
> a form which may be anything from a pentagon to an octagon, according to the number
> of dancers. This is called the Lock or Nut, which probably means Knot, and at Whitby
> the rose. In Shetland it was the Shield. It is the Glass of the Revesby play. The Lock,
> when formed, is variously treated. It may be laid on the ground, or raised breast-high or
> overhead, by the dancers as a body, or by their leader alone.

See also Cawte, Helm, and Peacock, *English Ritual Drama: A Geographical Index*, 37,
describing the defining characteristic of a Sword Dance: 'A man is executed by the lock of
swords round his neck, and is revived by either a doctor, a Clown, or a "Female."'

as the crest gets the voice right by proxy,[123]
non-stick like a teflon throat.[124] To press on
without fear of explanation, refusing the jab:
Ah Curly do your day is done,[125] *The course*   15
of woe is quickly run.[126] *Low without loss*[127]
your shining heart Has nothing but the better
part.[128] The star of swords is put upon
his neck. He falls to the ground.[129] Why not?
It is a root and branch arrangement,[130] giving   20

---

[123] Whilst 'proxy' need not have derived from *The Times* and is, in any case, a term associated with general elections via the established system of postal and proxy voting, it is nevertheless the case that *The Times* often printed notices of company meetings in this period in which shareholders' entitlement to 'vote by proxy' is advertised. See, for example, 'Annual Meeting of Stockholders, BASF '87', *The Times*, 15 May 1987, 22: 'Shareholders have the right to vote by proxy.'

[124] The 'non-stick' properties of polytetrafluoroethylene, branded and popularly known as Teflon, were frequently associated in the 1980s with the character and presidency of Ronald Reagan; the Democratic Representative Pat Schroeder is popularly credited with coining the epithet 'Teflon-coated presidency' in 1983. *The Times* refers to the epithet, or variations thereon, in at least eight articles between 1984 and 1987.

[125] The phrase 'day is done', and variations thereon, has hymnal, poetical, and proverbial histories and associations. See, for example, Julian, ed., *A Dictionary of Hymnology*, which cites six different first lines (either originally English or in translation from German or Greek) beginning 'The day is done' (1462), and further examples of the phrase besides (e.g., 'At evening time, when day is done', 88), as well as variations such as 'The day is gone' (seven instances, 1462). All of the published English usages of 'The day is done' in Julian's edition are predated by Henry Wadsworth Longfellow's poem 'The Day Is Done' (1844), though in hymnology the phrase 'Der Tag ist hin' is already well established in the seventeenth- and eighteenth-century German tradition.

[126] See the nineteenth-century English translation of Wagner's libretto to *Tristan und Isolde*, 3.4: 'In haste to wed / thee to my hero / with flying sails / I followed thy track: / but howe'er can / happiness / o'ertake the swift course of woe?' Wagner, *Tristan und Isolde*, 35.

[127] See George Herbert's 'Providence': 'Light without winde is glasse: warm without weight / Is wooll and furres: cool without closeness, shade: / Speed without pains, a horse: tall without height, / A servile hawk: low without losse, a spade.' Herbert, *The Temple*, 112.

[128] See Shakespeare, *1 Henry IV* (5.4, 'The better part of valour is discretion, in the which better part I have saved my life') and Augustine, *The City of God* ('the better part of every living creature, that is, the soul', 370).

[129] These lines describe the 'ritual killing' of the Sword Dance, a feature of the Revesby Play; see Chambers, *The English Folk-Play*, 110–12 (e.g., '*Then The Fool, kneeling down, with the swords round his neck ...*' (110) and '*Then, the dancers [putting] their swords round the Fool's neck again*' (111)). For a full explanation of the variations on the Sword Dance's ritual dramatic action, see Helm, *The English Mummers' Play*, 19–27. For the exact wording adapted by Prynne, see Cawte, Helm, and Peacock, *English Ritual Drama: A Geographical Index*, 37, describing a variation on the Sword Dance in some plays: 'The star of swords is put round the neck of a performer as in [the Sword Dance], and he may fall to the ground, but the action is carried no further, and there is no revival.' The feature described here does not apply to the Revesby Play, in which the Fool revives immediately after his 'execution'.

[130] See Phillips, 'Taking Stocks to Stores', 12 (image caption): 'High street stock market: The money shop in Debenhams' Bristol branch, bringing City business to the grass roots.'

the keys[131] openly to a provident reversal,[132]
to net uptake. To these Whom we resist.[133]
To blot out a shabby record by a daze
intrinsic in transit: *See what is won,*
We have cut him down, Like the evening sun[134]   25
His only crown.[135] Don't you think that's enough
to peel a larynx at a flotation, they say,[136]
by the stub of a tuning fork delivery. The issue
hits all-time peaks in no time at all,[137]
buy on the rumour, sell on the fact.[138] Only   30
a part gives access to the rest, you get
in at the floor too: *And his dance is gone.*[139]

It might justifiably be argued that this poem is more source than poem. The poem explicitly courts identification as a composite of linguistic objects through

---

[131] See Matthew 16:19, but more specifically, see Potter, *The English Morality Play*, 249n23: 'Based on the words of Christ to Peter, "And I will give to thee the keys of the kingdom of heaven, and whatsoever thou shalt bind on earth, it shall be bound in heaven: and whatsoever thou shalt loose on earth it shall be loosed also in heaven", Matthew xvi:19.'

[132] For 'provident', see Note 127, and Note 133 for its 'reversal' ('contrary to his high will').

[133] See *Paradise Lost*: 'Whereto with speedy words th'Arch-Fiend replied: / "Fall'n Cherub, to be weak is miserable, / Doing or suffering: but of this be sure, / To do aught good never will be our task, / But ever to do ill our sole delight, / As being the contrary to his high will / Whom we resist.' Milton, *Poetical Works*, 216. The words 'To these' appear in the Argument to book 1, in the following context: 'Satan awakens all his legions, who lay till then in the same manner confounded. They rise: their numbers, array of battle, their chief leaders named, according to the idols known afterwards in Canaan and the countries adjoining. To these Satan directs his speech . . .' (211–12).

[134] See Chambers, *The English Folk-Play*, 112: '*Then The Fool falls down, and the dancers, with their swords in their hands, sings the following song:* Good people all, you see what we have done: / We have cut down our father like ye evening sun, / And here he lies all in his purple gore, / And we are afraid he never will dance more.' See also p. 40 for a variation on this lament: 'See what I have done, / I have cut him down like the evening sun.'

[135] See Frederick William Orde Ward's 'The Tree of Death': 'In the dead of the night the Christ came down, / To visit the earth He made; / And a cross of care was His only crown, / As He stood in the heart of a mighty Town, / In the dread of the prison shade.' Ward, *'Twixt Kiss and Lip; or, Under the Sword*, 639.

[136] For 'flotation', see Poole, 'NFC Board Seeks Flotation Mandate', 19: 'The board of the National Freight Consortium, which was privatized in 1982 in an employee-led buyout, plans to seek a mandate from the group's 21,000 shareholders at the next annual meeting to float the company on the Stock Exchange – but only when the directors consider the timing is right.'

[137] See Tate and Smith, 'Shares Peak on Poll News', 19: 'Stock market records tumbled again yesterday as share prices responded spectacularly to the general election news. Both main share indices established new all-time peaks, even though by the close they were way below their best.'

[138] Ibid.: '"The markets appear to have been following the rule of buy on the rumour, sell on the fact", said Mr David Mission, international economist at Goldman Sachs'.

[139] See Chambers, *The English Folk-Play*, 112 (immediately following the Fool's 'execution' in the lines quoted in Note 134): '*Fool rises from the floor and says:* [*Fool.*] No, no, my children! by chance you are all mistaen! / For here I find myself, I am not slain; / But I will rise, your sport then to advance, / And with you all, brave boys, I'll have a dance.'

its selective italicization and irregular capitalization. It is more immediately obviously a collage than any of the poems in *The Oval Window*, though like the earlier sequence its collaged materials are arranged according to an original grammatical/linguistic totality that preserves, for the most part, an underlying, normative relationality between word, clause, line, and phrase. Lines 15–18 and 24–6 draw further attention to the poem's bricolage through their blending together of textual materials according to a tetrametrical (15–18) or dimetrical (24–6) ballad line, in each case the line breaks and capitalization serving to heighten the metrical division and subdivision.

The directional dynamics of the poem's textual materials, both found and originally composed, have been described by Ian Patterson as consisting of 'parallel notions of upness and downness', such as 'Death (or pseudo-death) and resurrection, collapse and cure, slump and recovery … high and low musical notes, valleys and peaks, tops and roots, and so on'.[140] The parallel dynamics that Patterson identifies are part of the poem's quote-driven systematicity: the peaks and troughs of the poem's lexical field evoke the real-time share price feeds of SEAQ, whilst the poem's newsprint sources tell a story about finance and political power that involves the infrastructural revolution of which SEAQ is a part. The major sources for this poem's collage are a series of articles from *The Times* (27–29 April 1987) describing the extension of share ownership amongst the British population (made possible in part by SEAQ); another from 12 May 1987 describing the spectacular effect on the stock market of Thatcher's announcement of the election date; and the text and scholarly accounts of the Revesby Play, a folk play of contested authenticity performed in Lincolnshire on 20 October 1779. The 'Fool' of the poem's title combines in one figure the stock Fool of the folk play tradition and the 'Greater Fool' of the investment theory of the same name, described in *The Times*. The inclusion in 'Fool's Bracelet' of Revesby Play material pertaining to the execution/ resurrection of the Fool (lines 18–19, 25, 32), whilst punning on the 'execution' of a trade, draws attention to an aspect of the play universal to such dramas, that is, a 'death and resurrection somewhere in the course of their action'.[141] In one of the studies of folk plays that Prynne read whilst composing 'Fool's Bracelet', the instrument and dramatic action of the Fool's execution, the 'star of swords', otherwise termed the 'lock', is interpreted according to its symbolic associations with the seasonal restoration of life, 'particularly if it [the lock] is taken as a symbol of the female principle placed over the head of a male performer to complete the union'.[142] Running through 'Fool's Bracelet', then, is

---

[140] Patterson, 'Fool's Bracelet', 51.   [141] Brody, *The English Mummers and Their Plays*, 3.
[142] Helm quoted in Brody, *The English Mummers and Their Plays*, 96.

a ritual drama of cyclical preservation, with the double figure of the Fool at its centre. By collaging this material alongside newspaper clippings about stock market fever at the prospect of another Tory government (lines 5–7, 29–30), the poem constructs a brief but ornate Miltonic satire of the national anticipation of Thatcher's third term, a satire that figures the incipient election ('the next round in the sing-song') as a popular drama that serves only to preserve life in the interests of a priestly caste of financiers and politicians.

The foolish citizen-subject of this drama is also directly implicated in the satire. On 28 April, *The Times* published the second of a three-part series of articles by Pearson Phillips about the 'new breed of shareholders' created through the recent flotations on the stock market of newly privatized companies (British Gas, British Telecom, and British Airways, amongst others).[143] All three articles are relevant to the subject matter of 'Fool's Bracelet', but the second article is crucial to the poem's conception and its organizing conceit. It describes the emergence of 'Share Shops' in the context of the 'alluring, heady world of modern money-culture', in effect detailing the consolidation of 'popular capitalism' as an ideological tenet and financial reality of Thatcher's second and third terms.[144] Phillips's subject is the Quilter Goodison Money Centre in the Bristol branch of the high street department store Debenhams, a photograph of which shows the Centre and some of its 'waiting clients'. The article ends with the following anecdote:

> Then something occurred which would have had the Chancellor, the Prime Minister, the chairman of the Stock Exchange and everyone else who professes to believe in wider share ownership dancing a jig of delight. A man arrived wearing a cloth cap. He was a worker in the pharmaceutical industry … He had bought [shares in] Wellcome when it came on to the market a year ago at 120. The screen showed it was now 284, well over double his money. He'd sell and switch to Beechams … In the space of around five minutes he had done his deals and departed. On the fourth floor of Bristol's Debenhams, at least, the age of Cloth-Cap Capitalism has arrived.[145]

This is a scene made possible by the infrastructural and technological developments exemplified by SEAQ, as Phillips's article shows: 'There are three television screens [in the Money Centre] and a couple of sharp young women ready to summon up any share price on the screen, linked to the Stock Exchange's SEAC [*sic*] system.'[146] The transformation of 'Cloth-Cap' subjects into financial actors which Phillips's article describes is taken up by Prynne's poem via the double figure of the eponymous Fool: by the inference of the

---

[143] 'Shares of the Cake', *The Times*, 27 April 1987, 1.
[144] Phillips, 'Taking Stocks to Stores', 12.   [145] Ibid.   [146] Ibid.

'Greater Fool' theory he, like the other 'waiting clients', is a patsy, beholden to the whims of the market, and ultimately a stooge acting in the interests of 'the Chancellor, the Prime Minister, [and] the chairman of the Stock Exchange'; by the inference of the Revesby material, he is a willing participant in a ritual drama of seasonal preservation and renewal, in this instance the renewal of Thatcherite political and economic power. Phillips's description of the Money Centre is that which 'Fool's Bracelet' figures, in its first three lines, in terms abstract enough to yield a metaphorical purchase on life as a fleeting asset in thrall to the market ('lifetime disposals') but closely enough yoked to its immediate inspiration ('shared', 'waiting clients') to act as a touchstone for the rest of the poem's roving associations.

The pseudo-allegorical abstraction of the opening lines' treatment of Phillips's scene allows for a broader sense to emerge of 'the waiting clients' as the UK electorate, whilst 'the day park shared by advancement' and the 'rising bunch of lifetime disposals' might be glossed as a withering description of contemporary citizenship, cynically patronized into class mobility by the appeal of financial agency. Such a political strategy was recognized at the time and written about in the left-wing press.[147] Lines 10–11's 'The upside of the song / from the valley below excites lock-tremors' sounds a variation on the same theme, as the siren song of profitable investment entices an inferred 'Cloth-Cap' yokel towards his own 'execution' (both in terms of a potential trade, an 'execution' he anticipates as a 'waiting client', and in terms of his sacrifice on the altar of capital). But the priorities of Prynne's versification are those of the collage as imitation screen market (Patterson's 'upness and down-ness'), rather than those of a narrative logic, so that the poem proceeds by associative linkage, internal cross-reference, and by replicating its lexical peaks and troughs ('rising bunch of lifetime disposals') throughout, arranging them around the central through line of the Revesby material and its permutations. The poem returns to an abstracted version of the Money Centre in the last three lines. The combination of newsprint ('buy on the rumour, sell on the fact') and metaphorical abstraction still recognizably in the purview of the subject of stocks, shares, and investment ('Only / a part gives access to the rest') combines here, as it does in the opening three lines, to pin the poem to its historical moment and to dramatize that moment through a figure of financialized self-hood: 'the floor' that 'you get / in at' is at once the shop floor of the Money Centre, the becoming-obsolete physical trading floor of the London Stock

---

[147] See, for example, Adam Raphael writing in *The Observer*, quoted in Hall, *The Hard Road to Renewal*, 88: 'It is estimated that the sell-off of British Gas [in 1986] will bring the number of individual shareholders in privatized companies to at least 6–10 million or an average of 10,000 to 15,000 voters in every constituency in the country with a financial stake in a Tory victory.'

Exchange, and the terminology for various types of lowest acceptable limit (of, for example, interest rates, or the value of a portfolio); what 'you get / in at', or what you are born into, is a financially and politically orchestrated *non plus ultra* of near-obsolete subjectivity. We saw in Section 3 how *The Oval Window* addresses the 'popular capitalism' latent in the privatization drives of Thatcher's second term through the poem's articulation of a privatized and financialized subjectivity. In 'Fool's Bracelet', we encounter a further develop-ment of this trend in the context of 'modern money-culture' and the transform-ation of political subjects into investing nodes in a financial–political nexus.

The poem's array of quoted, semi-quoted, and adapted source material also invokes Christian spirituality, eternity, and providence in ways that deepen and extend the satirical associations between the Revesby material and the vested financial/political interests that serve as the poem's implied 'elect'. The half-line quoted from Herbert's 'Providence', for example, is part of a stanza in the original poem emphasizing the bounty of God's immanence by reference to the harmonious suitability for their purpose of everyday objects (in Herbert's subsequent stanza, the implication of providential design is extended to the world of global commerce); 'a spade' is 'low without losse' because it allows man to reap the fruits of the earth with ease and furthermore infers the promise of resurrection through Christ. '*Low without loss*' is inserted by Prynne into the first of 'Fool's Bracelet's 'sing-song' balladic sections (lines 15–18), followed by '*your shining heart Has nothing but the better / part*': their collage implies that you find your providential suitability of purpose in the financial–political cycle which is the ideological arbiter of your needs and desires, whilst their stitched-together syntax ensures the implication is visibly *constructed*, the claim to spiritual commensurability audibly and visually undercut by the obviously manufactured textuality. Elements of Matthew 16:19 and half-lines cut and pasted from *Paradise Lost* are inset in lines 18–22. Their recombined syntax strongly suggests the passage is an explanation of, or commentary upon, the Revesby/Sword Dance material immediately preceding it, drawing the entire structure of the Revesby material's election satire to a point of summative declaration. The idiomatic 'root and branch' is given a further inflection from its source in the *Times* article on the QGC Money Centre, in the caption to its accompanying image: 'The money shop in Debenham's Bristol branch, bring-ing City business to the grass roots.'

The 'root and branch arrangement' diagrams the recomposition of political subjects into stakeholders with a financial interest in their own domination, through a polyvalent syntagm reminiscent of Herbert's predilection for suggest-ive condensation. That such an 'arrangement' entails 'giving / the keys openly to a provident reversal' implies that the power of the priestly financial and political elite already implicated in the poem's satire is the 'reversal' of a 'provident' financial arrangement, such as a credit union, but also that such power is given to a 'reversal' characterized as 'provident', that is, such power is transferred *from* the financial and political elite *to* the citizen-investors who, by their 'net uptake' of British Gas or Rolls-Royce shares, become the self-interested financiers of their future. The Yeats and Herbert quotations also directly contribute to the sense of the poem's lexical screen market – composed of various forms of highs and lows ('grief'/'joy', *'Low without loss'*) – and the juxtaposition of scripture and the canonical poets Yeats, Herbert, and Milton in the same poem as Frederick Ward proposes another version of the same comparative logic (i.e., major and minor). The Yeats and Herbert material furthermore contributes to the poem's thematic concern with trade and exchange, whilst the quotation from Matthew concretizes the implication of financial priestcraft made by the Revesby material as election satire. These interrelated aspects of some of the collaged quotations in 'Fool's Bracelet' go some way to describing the deep structure of the poem's intensely polysemous collage method, a method that proliferates associative networks between the lexical elements of the poem, as if circulating, or laundering, their associations through ritual, theatrical, financial, political, and spiritual channels.

The arrangement, adaptation, and traversal of the collaged elements in 'Fool's Bracelet', as well as mimicking the highs and lows of the SEAQ screen market, indicate the structure of another form of English folk drama, the medieval English morality play. From the 'waiting clients' eager to dispose of their savings on the stock market, to the Fool's '[fall] to the ground' after his 'execution', to the final reference to the *'dance'* (that is, in the Revesby Play, the dramatic correlate of his resurrection), Prynne's poem is arranged according to the tripartite structure of the morality play's 'sequence of innocence/fall/redemption', albeit with an additional, visible negation of the celebration of resurrection in the Revesby Play (the *'dance is gone'*).[148] The life cycle expressed through this sequence in the morality play's dramatic structure, writes Robert Potter, 'celebrate[s] the permanent truth of Christianity as a theology, a theory of history, and an explanation of the human condition'.[149] All the elements of 'Fool's Bracelet' examined here serve to construct a satirical diorama in miniature of just such an ontotheological principle: the poem is a verbal dramaturgy in screen-based bricolage of financial market theology. It is also a joke about the election, though a joke that by the nature of its composition makes some pointed claims about the intersecting forms of power and class interest that shape a parliamentary election's dramatic pretence of choice and

---

[148] Potter, *The English Morality Play*, 8.   [149] Ibid.

representation. The poem collages together finance and religion to satirize a political order that celebrates finance's leverage over policy, public discourse, and class interests through a quasi-religious appeal to the economy's onto-logical and temporal primacy. The poem's versification imitates the visual totality of the screen market, but its coerced eloquence as a whole poem – especially when read straight through and not studied in lexical isolation – sounds a song of domination, one composed through the polyphony of vested interests around the figure of the titular Fool, at once the victim of an inexorable fate and the 'client' of his own privatized self-interest. It is not a poem of anything like direct protest against the domination it dramatizes; the Fool is not a figure for an exploited mass, or even a person, but a stupidly complicit character on the stage of political economy. Such an approach certainly refuses, if only by contrarian satire, the liberal humanist reaction to the whole trajectory of Thatcherite social and economic reform as a perversion of putatively com-mon social values, or a falsification of all that was good and true under the post-war settlement. But the poem's critique of the ruling order seems itself to be pinioned to the ideological precepts of the latest cycle of accumulation, and its vision of a financialized subject might well be taken as a solely imitative elaboration of capital's reconfiguration of the relationship between information and value.

Joseph Vogl's theory of this reconfiguration since the early 1970s suggests that:

> By articulating the vision that all events and relationships in the world around us can be assigned a market value – in a perfectly competitive world we only need to know the price of things – the new liberalism implied that a differentiated, quasi-molecular market can safeguard every possible future with securities, options, and derivatives and so reinstate a kind of earthly Providence.[150]

'Fool's Bracelet' risks articulating the 'vision' that Vogl describes through a collage form so crammed with nested referential fields and ornately cross-pollinated networks of textual information that the collage becomes nothing more than a 'quasi-molecular market' of literary reference, its representation of the political order an obnoxiously complicated ventriloquism of the same political unfreedom to which it remains beholden. If, as Leigh Claire La Berge argues convincingly, 'an era of financialization is defined by the assump-tion of finance to a site of representational dominance', is not a collage aesthetic like Prynne's, with its constant re-presentation of its component parts, more

---

[150] Vogl, *The Specter of Capital*, 79.

than anything else another cultural symptom, however antagonistic, of that same dominance?[151] Whether any lyric personality or affective generosity might offer anything beyond an arbitrary reflection, from the vividly self-conscious to the flatly complicit, of the ever-mutating complexity of the systems of domination in which the subject of late, financialized capitalism might find themselves, is certainly not something that Prynne's poetry has ever had much interest in exploring, at least since the 1960s. Prynne's refusal of the potentialities of this approach has impelled his poetry towards the radical formal economy of the post-1980s work and contributed to the pointillistic dispersal of the language that characterizes his most recent poetry. Part of Douglas Oliver's response to Prynne's poems of the 1980s was to caution, in correspondence with Prynne, 'that the mere delineation of problems can seem defeating'; how, asks Oliver, does Prynne intend his poetry to 'lead out of the critique' it so exorbitantly mounts?[152] In Oliver's own poetry, it is the emblematic lyric voice of the poet-speaker that is the crucible of political agency, ethical indeterminacy, and social dialectic all at once; in Prynne's work, the only intimation of fellow feeling or shadow of lyric consolation comes in the form exemplified by the acidly ironic 'day park shared by advancement', a diurnal boundary of mutual existence, its 'natural' limit and extension divided ('shared') according to the financial principle which binds the 'waiting clients' – and 'you' – to its 'floor'.

Oliver's question is posed in the context of a twenty-year-old correspondence and long-standing mutual appreciation, which sharpens rather than diminishes its challenge to Prynne's poetry and poetics. The challenge is a familiar one in radical and experimental literary, philosophical, and activist circles and has been for a long time. Its implied criticism – that Prynne's work develops an account of the social, cultural, and political organs of contemporary life that is finally aporetic, not leading a way 'out' but more and more consumed with the detail of the 'problems' – also resonates with the history of twentieth-century critical theory and is reminiscent, for example, of Habermas's frustration with, and refutation of, earlier Frankfurt School critiques of instrumental reason developed by Horkheimer, Adorno, and Marcuse.[153] The essence of Oliver's challenge, however, has less to do with the legacy of instrumental reason than with a practical concern that poetry maintain an ethical imperative towards

---

[151] La Berge, *Scandals and Abstraction*, 30.

[152] Oliver to Prynne, 2 November 1987. J. H. Prynne Papers.

[153] See, for example, Seyla Benhabib's sympathetic account of Habermas's project in *Critique, Norm, and Utopia*, 224–78.

a better future, a concern that is legible across practically everything Oliver wrote, and which is the subject of a great deal of his correspondence with Prynne. Prynne's reply to the letter in which Oliver poses his question responds sceptically to Oliver's faith in basic human decency (what Oliver calls in his letter 'the prudence of the human heart') more than it does to the specific caution against critical aporia, in effect substituting a refutation of Oliver's path 'out of the critique' for an explanation of his own work's guiding principles. But a simple answer to Oliver's challenge would be that Prynne's poetry (certainly of the period, though arguably across the *oeuvre*) is far more interested in finding new ways *into* the 'problems' it articulates than it is in finding ways 'out' of them.

The priorities of the poetry, as I have argued, are those of knowledge sought within and across a multiplicity of technical, ideological, and political orders of understanding and justification, such that the poem entails a lexical traversal of those orders (serial and constellatory in the case of *The Oval Window*, pressurized and archly satirical in the case of *Bands around the Throat*). Unlike Oliver's poetry, Prynne's poetry does not nominate any threshold of moral or ontological achievement as that which could be realized in social life, or even grasped by the intellect, in response to the recalibration of political and economic life in the United Kingdom in the 1980s. Yet if Prynne's poetry of the period approaches a kind of zero-degree rendition of financial ideology, it does so by composing its vision through a collage method that foregrounds the very historical depth and complexity that such an ideology renders infinitely one-dimensional (according to the providence of market rationality); if the poetry fashions a teeming, verbal image of a moment of depthless contemporaneity inspired by the appresentational simultaneity of the screen market, that image seeks to interrupt as much as to 'delineate' its present moment, through a vocabulary which overwhelmingly intensifies and proliferates historical perspective. And if, as Vogl suggests, financialization seeks the end of history in the interests of accumulation, poems like 'Fool's Bracelet' proliferate a comparative knowledge perversely unredeemable according to the market structures that they satirize. Just as the serial development of *The Oval Window* maintains an uneven anti-systematicity that is the poem's dynamic, dissonant counterpart to the privatized subject's 'infinite linear address space', so the poems in *Bands around the Throat* perform an imaginative historicization of the matter of economic eternity. Their collages interleave in dynamic contradiction what Vogl, in his meta-history of finance, calls 'historical time' – 'full, concrete, particular, irreversible, and limited' – within and against the 'chrematistic striving' of 'economic time', the 'measureless, empty, indeterminate, proleptic, and abstract' time of the market.[154] The end of 'Fool's Bracelet' is both the indication of resurrection/renewal according to the life cycle of the providential, neoliberal political–financial nexus and the vanishing point of its internal temporal logic as an eternal absence: '*And his dance is gone*'. But the poem as a whole is composed according to a collage method that militates against this eternal absence with every cross-reference and nested evocation of textual and historical significance.

'Almost Lunch-Time' is composed along similar lines:[155]

Almost Lunch-Time

Or, like two-shoes on a revised citation
    the master of these powers to afflict[156]
instantly cries up the residue, at a speed[157]
    divested of charm. You get to go

Over-the-shoulder but with your ankle flexed,[158]   5
    on and on if not right back
at the start line around the chicken factory,[159]
    where was a sugar and fretty.[160]

---

[154] Vogl, *The Specter of Capital*, 127.   [155] Prynne, *Poems*, 354.

[156] For 'the master of these powers', see Dorner, *History of Protestant Theology*, 362–4, paraphrasing Schelling: 'He [Schelling] insists upon a history of mankind, a history ruled by providence; but the history of the world is to him at the same time the history of God . . . Thus it is by means of an historical process that human nature, which had fallen a victim to the subversion of the powers of nature, becomes, through the agency of the second potency in man and his reaction, the master of these powers through culture.' For 'afflict', see *Timon of Athens*, 4.2: 'My dearest lord, blessed to be most accursed, / Rich only to be wretched, thy great fortunes / Are made thy chief afflictions' (see Note 167).

[157] The phrase 'to cry up' has a history of usage in specifically economic terms (often in association with currency and credit) as in the historical examples given by the *Oxford English Dictionary* (*OED*): 'When your credit it cryed up to the highest' (1631) and 'Crying up the pieces of Eight' (?1673).

[158] To look over one's left shoulder is, in traditional song, a sign of imminent bad news or the confirmation of the same. Examples include 'The Bold Prisoner' (Roud no. 83), 'Geordie' (Roud no. 90), and 'Johnie Armstrong' (Roud no. 76, and interpolated in Prynne's 'Marzipan', from *Bands around the Throat*). The connotations of bad luck that have accrued to all things 'left' derive from the etymology of 'sinister', through Anglo-Norman, Middle French, and Latin, as *OED* details.

[159] See Campbell, 'Unigate in £55m Chicken Scheme', 23: 'Unigate, the expanding milk, meat and food producing group, yesterday put up a "for sale" sign over its five engineering businesses and revealed a £55 million investment in a chicken-rearing and processing plant in South Humberside . . . Stock market reaction to Unigate's decision to shed its engineering interests, which only accounted for 5 per cent of group operations, was to mark the shares up from 413p to 424p at one stage.'

[160] See Halliwell, *The Nursery Rhymes of England*, 212: 'Where was a sugar and fretty? / And where was jewel and spicy? / Hush-a-bye, babe in a cradle, / And we'll go away in a tricy!'

There is no alarm at the menu of constraints[161]
    as the bills mount in the pre-tax void,[162]   10
all our bills grinding by the dream of friendship[163]
    in double running, cloud filling,[164]

The drone of faster upturn.[165] Fresh denials
    clothe the bare strip in verdure
and smiles in the street. Thus seen when said,[166]   15
    undone by goodness not waiting,[167]

When therefore sleep and take your cut,[168]
    distressed by patience: 'it is difficult
to learn to perform ethically'.[169] Stupidly good[170]
    as a standing order the new figures   20

Bear out the old question, as next to go
    with all her rings and all her show[171]

---

[161] See Mathewson and Winter, 'The Economics of Vertical Restraints in Distribution', 212: 'Antitrust policy in the United States and other countries towards vertical restrictions on distribution (restrictions placed by manufacturers on retailers' prices and quantities), has been fragmented and unsettled ... Section II of this chapter sets out the menu of constraints we wish to consider, together with a synthesis of previous analyses of these restraints.'

[162] See 'Impressive Start by New CE Heath Management', *The Times*, 22 May 1987, 24: 'After £11 million of provisions for bad debts and litigation, pretax profits more than halved last year from £34.7 million to £14.5 million.'

[163] See Ward, 'Day Calls for Morals in Business', 25, quoting Graham Day, chairman of the Rover Group: 'However, life is not always that clear-cut and it is the marginal decisions, where we get sucked in by life's dreams, that I think test us.'

[164] The terms 'double running' and 'cloud filling' are the names of stitches in embroidery.

[165] For 'upturn' see Smith, 'Industry Investment Dips by 3%', 23: 'The weakness of investment, alongside a rapid recovery in output, casts doubts on whether industry will have sufficient capacity to cope with a sustained upturn.'.

[166] The half-line 'Thus seen when said' recalls Samuel Beckett's roughly contemporaneous *Ill Seen Ill Said* (1981).

[167] See *Timon of Athens*, 4.2: 'Poor honest lord, brought low by his own heart, / Undone by goodness! Strange unusual blood / When man's worst sin is he does too much good.'

[168] See Cicero (*De divinatione ad Brutum*) quoted in Chroust, *Aristotle*, 379: 'When, therefore, sleep has freed the intellect (the mind, or the soul) from its association and contact with the body, it remembers the past, discerns the present and foresees the future. For the body of a sleeping man lies like that of a dead man, but his mind is active and alive.'

[169] See Ward, 'Day Calls for Morals in Business', 25: 'He [Day] said graduates must also have a good standard of moral values because it was difficult to learn to perform ethically in the business world.'

[170] See Milton, *Poetical Works*, 381: 'That space the Evil One abstracted stood / From his own evil, and for the time remained / Stupidly good, of enmity disarmed, / Of guile, of hate, of envy, of revenge; / But the hot hell that always in him burns, / Though in mid-heav'n, soon ended his delight'.

[171] See 'The Gypsy Countess' (a variation of Roud no. 1) in Baring-Gould, Sheppard, and Bussell, *Songs of the West*, 103: 'They sang so sweet; they sang so shrill, / That fast her tears began to flow. / And she laid down her silken gown, / Her golden rings, and all her show'.

out along that road; beating their best
back into bounds,[172] the near-perfect rest.[173]

Like 'Fool's Bracelet', this poem is composed using newsprint from *The Times* (22 May 1987), quotation (in this case from a single source) that pertains, in its original context, to providence (J. A. Dorner's *History of Protestant Theology* (1871)), and quotation of, or allusion to, folk literature and lore (folk song, nursery rhyme, and the practice of 'beating the bounds'). The poem establishes fewer internal cross-references than 'Fool's Bracelet', but its collage creates a similar matrix of subtextual inference and association. The title's evocation of the middle of the working day sets up a conceptual perimeter (recalling the 'day park' of 'Fool's Bracelet') within which economic and traditional boundaries, providential order and profiteering, and divination and ethical performance are spliced together. Economic, monetary, and market terminology or allusion structure the poem from start to finish: the phrasal verb 'cries up' (recalling its usages in relation to currency and credit and its echo of the term 'open outcry', the pre–screen market method of traders' communication on the exchange floor), 'pre-tax void', 'drone of faster upturn', 'take your cut', a quotation from the chairman of the Rover Group, Graham Day (lines 18–19), 'standing order', the quotations from *Timon of Athens* (lines 2 and 16, about Timon's profligacy), and a paper on 'The economics of vertical restraints in distribution' (line 9, 'menu of constraints'). The syntactical integration of this diction with the folk material in the collage – lines 5, 8, and especially the final reference to 'beating the bounds' (lines 23–4) – embeds economic logics and market rationality within the organic cultural practices of the population. It also suggests an ethical paradigm, native to economic theory, which begins with the inherent 'goodness' of riches and their distribution (the cipher for which is the figure of Timon), and for which welfare is a measurable quantity belonging to consumers, and thus a function of consumption (the assumption written into the scholarly paper on vertical restraints).

---

[172] The phrase 'beating the bounds' refers to a specific rural tradition of demarcating parish borders. See Oliver, '"Beating the Bounds": Switching Boundaries over Five Millennia'. See also Mathewson and Winter, 'The Economics of Vertical Restraints in Distribution', 226: 'If the retail market is an infinite line, there are always consumers located directly at an outlet in the non-integrated equilibrium who are located arbitrarily close to a market boundary in the integrated equilibrium – i.e., who pay the highest delivered price.' See also the poem 'Fresh Running Water' in *Bands around the Throat* (*Poems*, 353): 'As we're all bound / to go that far, we beat our way over / the bright track to the billet there.'

[173] See Dorner, *History of Protestant Theology*, 364, paraphrasing Schelling: 'The certainty, however, of that perfection which is ever realizing something higher than that which previously existed, shows that God ever remains master of these His potencies, although He actually suffers Himself to be in a state of struggle.'

'Almost Lunch-Time' is framed by quotation of, and allusion to, a summary of Schelling's late thought, from Dorner's *History*. This is the source of the first stanza's 'master of these powers' and the text to which the last stanza's 'near-perfect rest' alludes. Schelling 'insists', writes Dorner, 'upon a history of mankind ... ruled by providence; but the history of the world is to him at the same time the history of God'.[174] After a description of Schelling's historico-theological system, according to which postlapsarian primitive man caused a universal disturbance through his 'setting free of the potency' of 'boundless being' preserved within him, Dorner writes that 'it is by means of an historical process that human nature, which had fallen victim to the subversion of the powers of nature, becomes, through the agency of the second potency in man and his reaction, the master of these powers through culture'.[175] Dorner concludes his summary of Schelling's late system with the following remark:

> The certainty, however, of that perfection which is ever realizing something higher than that which previously existed, shows that God ever remains master of these His potencies, although He actually suffers Himself to be in a state of struggle.[176]

The final two stanzas of 'Almost Lunch-Time' quote Cicero's *De divinatione*, a *Times* report on the Rover Group chairman's call 'for morals in business', Milton (again), and the folk song 'The Gypsy Countess'; they also refer to the practice of 'beating the bounds' and, through the final line's 'the near-perfect rest', to Dorner's 'that perfection which is ever realizing something higher than that which previously existed'. The lines are plaintive but mock-commiserative, their cadence tending towards condescension rather than pity, as if placating a child; they seem to reassure the one enjoined to 'sleep and take your cut' that the 'new figures / Bear out the old question', that what has been will be and always will do, a reassurance built on the collage's recombinant proposal of financial divination, folksy familiarity, and the wretchedly ironic coincidence of ethical performance with market rationality ('it is difficult / to learn to perform ethically') as the beating heart of popular capitalism. The logic of this reassurance, the provenance of 'Stupidly good' suggests, is essentially satanic – cunning, deceptive, and morally bankrupt – and runs as follows: contemporary *Homo economicus* achieves a 'near-perfect rest' (as opposed to the 'state of struggle' suffered by Schelling's God) because the boundary beaten into him, and which defines his existence in relation to the future, is the 'drone of faster upturn' itself, the monotonous inertia of an economic time that has assumed the providential mantle of world history under the sign of perfect competition.

---

[174] Dorner, *History of Protestant Theology*, 362.   [175] Ibid., 362–4.   [176] Ibid., 364.

Another poem in *Bands around the Throat*, 'No Song No Supper', makes explicit that such inertia is objectified by the appresentational, scopic medium of the screen market, just as it was subjectivized by the 'vantage, private and inert' in *The Oval Window*: 'For here is the display now, of inert / promise like a flick-knife in milk / dipping and turning to catch the offer'.[177] The last stanza of 'Almost Lunch-Time' dutifully comes to rest in a double-couplet of end-rhymes that are, in part, the sounding out of a formal boundary as an aural image of self-referential, and self-reproducing, eternity. But through the common-place, phonetic materiality which is the substance of their aural consonance, these last, flagrantly innocuous rhymes surely also point to something beyond themselves, if only to that very phonetic materiality which renders them at once simply innocuous and so, at the end of a poem of such overtly complex ways of meaning, also highly suspect. To end a poem like 'Almost Lunch-Time' with a rhyme on the word ('rest') that is at the heart of the poem's impression of economic 'secular eternity' and its claims on the inertial present is to insist on the contingency of that futurity by a small but resonant claim on the agility and depth of poetical language to evade and outflank the 'drone of faster upturn' to which it refers. The end-rhymes of the final stanza snatch a moment of fugitive pleasure from the maw of the 'near-perfect rest' which they signify. They are a vivid instance of the historicizing sabotage attempted by the lexical, referen-tial, and associative networks that compose *Bands around the Throat*'s portfolio of strangled songs.

5 Somewhere Else

Six months after the publication of *Bands around the Throat*, Prynne wrote a letter to Douglas Oliver that situates both poets' work in relation to their contemporaries recently selected by Andrew Crozier and Tim Longville for the anthology *A Various Art* (1987), in which Oliver and Prynne are substantially represented. The letter is vituperative about Crozier's editorial introduction, which begins with the following claim:

> This anthology represents our joint view of what is most interesting, valuable, and distinguished in the work of a generation of English poets now entering its maturity, but it is not an anthology of English, let alone British poetry.[178]

---

[177] Prynne, *Poems*, 343.

[178] Crozier and Longville, eds., *A Various Art*, 11. Crozier's argument is that the poetry represented in the anthology is antipathetic towards (or simply uninterested in) the sense of 'prestige of national origin' and the 'Imperial suitings' of the poetry that laid claim to a national literary art in the 1950s, by which he means (but does not name as such) the anti-modernist poets of, or affiliated with, the Movement group.

This, felt Prynne, was tantamount to a betrayal of the breadth of engagements with the deep questions of 'national life and language' that had been steadily and wilfully practised by the anthologized poets since the late 1960s:

> Who in the name of F.T. Palgrave asked [Crozier] to pre-warn readers of this book that the work to follow does not form part of the national poetry of Britain? That somehow the poets they agreed to include have been success-fully elbowed aside by a bit of tinpot literary history and a few bored metropolitan publishers? Does he not observe the question of national life and language, the 'condition of England' indeed, being continually and strongly addressed from a whole series of positions within the scales of chronology and individual leverage? ... This defensive title that they have chosen, for a book I incline to believe they have not read, obscures the fact that a more proper caption would have been *English Poetry and the Poetry of England, 1960–1985*.[179]

Prynne's 'more proper caption' is itself inaccurate, not least because not all the poets assembled in *A Various Art* were English. Veronica Forrest-Thompson was born in British Malaya and raised in Glasgow; Iain Sinclair is, and John James was, Welsh; John Hall was born in 1945 in what was then Northern Rhodesia and moved to England in 1958; Oliver himself was raised in England by Scottish Presbyterian parents (and often emphasized this aspect of his heritage). Prynne's chagrin at the editors' implied refutation of the 'question of national life and language' that he, at least partly, projects onto the anthology, would seem to stem from a perceived misrecognition by the editors of his own poetry's priorities. The 'question of national life' was certainly a priority recognized and shared by Oliver; less than a month earlier, he had written to Prynne that *Bands around the Throat* 'clings ... to the process of modern Britain', a process which Oliver himself had spent six years (1979–85) meticu-lously satirizing in his dream vision *The Infant and the Pearl* (1985, excerpted in *A Various Art*).[180]

In what sense, then, are *The Oval Window* and *Bands around the Throat* distinctly British books of poetry? How do they 'observe the question of national life and language' and the 'condition of England'? They do so by articulating, through their collage method, a vision of the country yoked to the governance and ideological influence of Thatcher's Conservatives, and also, especially in *Bands around the Throat*, by responding to the international structures and contexts of capital accumulation and circulation that bred, and were intensified by, successive Tory governments' umbilical relationship with the City of London. If we consider the poetry in Prynne's 1980s books as

---

[179] Prynne to Oliver, 30 November 1987. J. H. Prynne Papers.
[180] Oliver to Prynne, 2 November 1987.

a distinctly national poetry, it is the poetry of a nation in despair: hammered into submission, privatized into limitless solipsism, and driven into the waiting arms of the manager of the Quilter Goodison Money Centre. The 'question of national life' in *The Oval Window* and *Bands around the Throat*, then, is not really a question of the lives of the nation's people, in the sense of their desires, or griefs, or fears, or loves. It is a question of the complexity, power, and coercion of the economic, ideological, and globally financial valuation of those lives; it is a question, too, of those lives' own stupefied capitulation to the forces that shape them, according to the moral and behavioural manipulation intrinsic to the synthetic drama of their existence. This is perhaps overstating the case, but it is worth overstating it to emphasize the ways in which Prynne's poetry of the period conceives of an attention to the 'real data' of national degradation (the 'attrition of the real', as his 17 July 1983 letter to Dorn has it) that would match in objective scope the hated litany of reportage in *The Times*, whilst subjecting that data to a poetical sabotage of their official terms of reference. The result is that Prynne's poems of the period aspire to a form of experimental enquiry – a 'scalpel of research', to borrow Dobran's term for the 1970s work – not just into the ruling political order but into the very substance of that order's designs on social reality: 'a kind of unofficial window into treasury policy', for example, or 'a part [that] gives access to the rest'. Not apart from, or outside of the market, but perpetually somewhere else inside it, the radical, perverse, and Poundian desire the poetry has is not to fashion a transcendent riposte to the news but to be quite literally in competition with it.

Prynne's 1987 letter to Oliver, despite its rancour about the editorial apparatus of *A Various Art*, is also a benediction on Oliver's recent engagement to the poet Alice Notley. It ends with a transcription of the Tudor song 'Smale pathis to the grenewode', after some reflection on the 'inset folksong in the recent texts' (i.e., *Bands around the Throat*):

> these voices are the victims, for sure, since the fair field is full of yuppies and agribrokers [*sic*], and Benjamin Britten (say) is not an option. But: the national poetry! The national language! 'I heard a maiden singing in the valley below' ... There is still a shimmer in the durable latency of the common rhymes, after so much has been done and undone, as if providence itself resided within these hazards of phonetic accident, in the distant burden within language of its own internal echo, these sounds are not quite erased from our current immunity to the recall of innocence tagged and destroyed.[181]

Prynne here quotes the same song ('Early One Morning') that he quoted in 'Fool's Bracelet', though he does not subject it in the letter to the same pressure

---

of dispersal into the ups and downs of the screen market as in the poem ('the upside of the song / from the valley below excites lock-tremors'). That the song is emblematic, in the letter, of the 'durable latency of the common rhymes' is surely evidence that what Prynne considered necessary to subject to a painfully satirical pressure in 'Fool's Bracelet' was not, therefore, exempt from exercising a profound and contradictory pressure of verity and fellow feeling against the 'yuppies and agribrokers' who are, in turn, the agents of that feeling's flotation on the stock market of national political discourse. Even 'providence' is recovered in the letter, briefly and conditionally ('as if'), from its imbrication, in the poems, into the scopic spread of the City's electronic Cassandras.

The letter is wistfully, even pedantically cautious in the manner in which it identifies 'the distant burden within language of its own internal echo', as though intellectually hypervigilant against a merely emotional appreciation of the simple beauty of traditional song. But such hypervigilance (which we might, more generously, read as improvisatory musing to a trusted friend) is also an indication of the extent to which Prynne prized songs like 'Smale pathis to the grenewode' and 'Early One Morning' for their capacity to fashion an audible threshold onto a horizon of meaning and social currency 'not quite erased' from a commons subjected to nearly a decade of the 're-educating attrition of the real' under Thatcher.[182] This threshold recalls the adventures in aural fantasy in *The Oval Window*, and indeed the 'national language' of traditional song takes on, in the letter, something of the fungible metonymy of the ear/*tz'u*/toy motif in that earlier poem. In light of this letter, moments such as the 'inset folksong' in 'Fool's Bracelet', and the all-too-human end-rhyme on 'rest' in 'Almost Lunch-Time', sound a soft, but distinctly emancipatory note, all the more resonant for their disciplined subjection to the formal imitation of the screen market. Prynne's unwavering focus on the 'attrition of the real' in this period, its nationalist idiom of economism and self-sufficiency, leaves little room for any indication of the myriad currents and movements of equally real social contestation of state power in the 1980s, from the Brixton riots, to the Battle of Orgreave, to the Greenham Common Women's Peace Camp. But what the poetry loses by these omissions is calculatedly offset by its determination to meet the 'attrition of the real' on the terms and terminology of its own economic and political domination and to make out of the inert matter of financial eternity

---

[182] Prynne's description of the 'inset folksong' in his poems resembles, in a kind of attenuated version, the far more optimistic account by Gerald Porter of Charles Dickens's practice of quoted song fragments: 'In making such rich allusion to songs [in his novels], Dickens restores to audibility those voices which had been reduced to a whisper in the nineteenth century, and whose silencing was necessary for the coherence of Victorian ideology.' See Constantine and Porter, *Fragments and Meaning in Traditional Song*, 188–221 (201).

an intensely historical field of 'internal echo[es]', a shifting, fugitive, audible image just shy of what might be called, somewhere else entirely, a substantive concept of utopia, ringing like tinnitus in the mind's ear.

The mind's ear has become the special focus of Prynne's thinking about poetry and knowledge in more recent years. The essay 'Mental Ears and Poetic Work' (2010) and the study of Wordsworth's poem 'The Solitary Reaper', *Field Notes: 'The Solitary Reaper' and Others* (2007), both develop accounts of poetic composition and reception that foreground poetry's capacity to produce encounters with the world that are undeceived by, because in full acknowledgement and even heightened cognizance of, the structural domination and inherent exploitation which determine social being and exchange in a class society. In each of these experimental prose works, Prynne identifies special kinds of audibility that enable and facilitate such encounters, and which generate through practised cultivation, he argues, a knowledge of the world that is essentially and profoundly truthful. In *Field Notes*, the fact that Wordsworth's poem is centred upon a scene of listening to a song that cannot be discerned in its linguistic specificity ('Will no one tell me what she sings?'), but the sound of which is nevertheless heard and attended to with deep and abiding attention and thoughtfulness, is that from which the poem derives its fundamental power, 'not delight merely but profound human truth in the focus of imagination'.[183] Because, in Prynne's account, 'the elemental power of simple reality would all too readily be buried by narratives of explanation and accommodation' that would impose a sentimental, philanthropic, or otherwise obscuring narrative framework upon the reaper's 'melancholy strain', it is only through what Prynne terms the 'audible song of [this strain's] muting' that the poem refuses to assimilate the sound of rural labour to the imaginative 'class-empowering immunity' of those (like Wordsworth) who are at leisure to think and write about it. In doing so, the poem creates the conditions for an ethically exacting intersubjectivity, such that 'the poet-traveller's focus of awareness can be projected right out into the field, into the resonant open space which is intermediate between singer and hearer and which is the place of unobstructed confluence of recognition'.[184]

In 'Mental Ears and Poetic Work', which also closely reads Wordsworth and which, unlike *Field Notes*, explicitly refers to Prynne's own practice and career of composition, Prynne suggests that a form of evolutionary phonology is the peculiar domain of what he calls 'poetic work'.[185] This work comprises writing and reading poetry, and in both cases it describes the active, focussed attention

---

[183] Prynne, *Field Notes*, 66.   [184] Ibid., 19, 135, 89.
[185] Prynne, 'Mental Ears and Poetic Work', 127.

of hearing what is in poems, particularly the kind of knowledge they contain or transmit. In his description of how the 'poet works with mental ears', Prynne describes the 'specialized audition' of the poet as peculiarly attuned to the 'sounds that poems make', such that 'the real-time sounds of speech and vocalized utterance are disintegrated into sub-lexical acoustic noise by analogy with the striking clatter of real work in the material world'.[186] What 'mental ears' can be trained to discern in order for poetry to do the work that it needs to do, suggests Prynne, are the ways in which poems are capable of disclosing (Prynne's verb) something of the 'evolutionary process in language history', the deep structure of historical time that shows through, and in, the changing sounds and part-meanings of the phonological record; poems disclose this process in dynamic relation to the formal features and accumulated histories of poetic composition (rhythm, assonance, all that stuff).[187] What 'mental ears' discern, ultimately, is the contradictory matter of that which poems are made of. Line breaks, for example, are a kind of 'prosodic breakage', involving an inherent movement of 'continuity by versus and retroflex', that, along with other formal features, '[disrupt] a complaisant surface harmony by head-on turns which generate energy of conception and conscience'.[188]

Here is a representative sample of 'Mental Ears':

> The very medium of poetic textuality incorporates and instantiates the fea-
> tures of breakage at local and microscopic levels, as discoverable by phono-
> logical and other types of analysis, into a dialectic which may look arbitrary
> or merely optional but which polarizes the task of poetic composition ... In
> these ways maybe it's possible and perhaps even obligatory to think with
> 'mental ears', focused on the fault-lines in language and thought as
> a discontinuous system upon the inevitable fault-lines in ethical being and
> in material reality ... Because active human knowledge is ... inherently
> dialectical and in dispute with itself and its base in reality, the apparently
> segregated domains of poetry turn out, by reverse transit through the mental
> ears, to connect at full intensity with the disorders of public conscience[.][189]

I introduce these late, experimental prose works to reflect, in conclusion, on the kinds of things that are going on in *The Oval Window* and *Bands around the Throat*. John Wilkinson has suggested that in 'issuing the Wordsworth commentary, Prynne presumably is making public in another register certain claims developed in his verse and identifiable there from the beginning'; the same suggestion might be made, even more easily, about 'Mental Ears'.[190] This does seem to me a presumption worth making (and in the case of 'Mental Ears' it is incontrovertibly accurate), though I would qualify Wilkinson's 'from the

---

[186] Ibid., 128, 130.   [187] Ibid., 137.   [188] Ibid., 140–1.   [189] Ibid., 141–2.
[190] Wilkinson, 'Heigh Ho: A Partial Gloss of *Word Order*', 298.

beginning', since this risks attributing to Prynne a sort of supra-conscious grasp of his poetics over many decades. What is certainly true, however, is that these late essays make public the mature poetry's motivated encounter with 'the fault lines' in the ethical and material basis of reality through the medium of a 'poetic textuality' – what I have been describing as the collage method of the 1980s work – trained on the 'attrition of the real' in its various guises, whether under the mantle of state recomposition (*The Oval Window*) or of financial providence (*Bands around the Throat*). But what the essays illuminate of the poetry's aspiration to the profoundest truth of encounter with the fabric of an exploitative reality comes at the cost of the no-less profoundly adversarial nature of that encounter in the poems. Audibility in the poetry is less 'specialized' than it is fantastical, or fugitive; it affords glimpses onto a synaesthetic, polyvocal stratum of emphatic humanity that operates against the grain of what is heard and seen through the leader columns, database systems, and share price listings of the United Kingdom. The knowledge that is produced in the poems is less essentially coeval with 'its base in reality', and thus also the 'disorders of public conscience' that it traces, than it is antagonistic towards the social metrics of what is rendered conscionable by the façade of public consent; instead of the 'unobstructed confluence of recognition' prized in *Field Notes*, the poems seek primarily to obstruct the lazy misrecognition of ideological confluence (of, for example, goodness and value). Prynne's poetry of the 1980s thinks through 'the fault-lines in language' about the 'fault-lines in ethical being and material reality', and does so through an assiduously historical, collage mentality. But the fault-lines that are discerned thereby are not therefore as 'inevitable' as they come to be in 'Mental Ears', because they are still the broken contours of a world thrown into relief by those entangled thresholds of euphonic audibility that figure the given future as less inevitable with every calculated strophe against the daily record of our present inhumanity.

References

'Annual Meeting of Stockholders, BASF '87'. *The Times* (London), 15 May 1987, 22.

Augustine. *The City of God against the Pagans*. Edited and translated by R. W. Dyson. Cambridge: Cambridge University Press, 1998.

Baring-Gould, S., H. Fleetwood Sheppard, and F. W. Bussell. *Songs of the West: Folk Songs of Devon and Cornwall, Collected from the Mouths of the People*. London: Methuen, [1905?].

Bellringer, Christopher, and Ranald Michie. 'Big Bang in the City of London: An Intentional Revolution or an Accident?'. *Financial History Review* 21, no. 1 (2014): 111–37.

Benhabib, Seyla. *Critique, Norm, and Utopia: A Study of the Foundations of Critical Theory*. New York: Columbia University Press, 1986.

Brody, Alan. *The English Mummers and Their Plays: Traces of Ancient Mystery*. London: Routledge and Kegan Paul, 1969.

C., J. 'Little Read Books'. *TLS* 5926 (October 2016). www.the-tls.co.uk/art icles/little-read-books/.

Cambridge University Library. 'Cambridge School Poets'. www .lib.cam.ac.uk/collections/departments/manuscripts-university-archives /significant-archival-collections/poetry.

Campbell, Colin. 'Unigate in £55 m Chicken Scheme'. *The Times* (London), 22 May 1987, 23.

Cawte, E. C., Alex Helm, and N. Peacock. *English Ritual Drama: A Geographical Index*. London: The Folk-Lore Society, 1967.

Cetina, Karin Knorr. 'From Pipes to Scopes: The Flow Architecture of Financial Markets'. *Distinktion: Scandinavian Journal of Social Theory* 4, no. 2 (2011): 7–23.

Cetina, Karin Knorr, and Alex Preda. 'The Temporalization of Financial Markets: From Network to Flow'. *Theory, Culture and Society* 24, no. 7/ 8 (2007): 116–38.

Chambers, E. K. *The English Folk-Play*. Oxford: Clarendon, 1933.

Chappell, W. *Popular Music of the Olden Time; a Collection of Ancient Songs, Ballads, and Dance Tunes, Illustrative of the National Music of England*. Vol. 2. London: Cramer, Beale, and Chappell, 1859.

Chroust, Anton-Hermann. *Aristotle: New Light on His Life and on Some of His Lost Works, Vol. 2: Observations on Some of Aristotle's Lost Works*. London: Routledge and Kegan Paul, 1973.

Clark, Michael. 'Election Date Lifts Shares to Two-Day Gain of £15bn'. *The Times* (London), 12 May 1987, 20.

Cohen, Michael C. 'Getting Generic: An Introduction'. *Nineteenth-Century Literature* 71, no. 1 (September 2016): 147–55.

Constantine, Mary-Ann, and Gerald Porter. *Fragments and Meaning in Traditional Song: From the Blues to the Baltic.* Oxford: Oxford University Press, 2003.

Cookson, Clive. 'Hattersley Formula for Equality'. *The Times* (London), 25 August 1983, 4.

Cowton, Rodney. 'Arms Spending Rises 19% under Tories'. *The Times* (London), 7 July 1983, 4.

Crozier, Andrew, and Tim Longville, eds. *A Various Art.* London: Carcanet, 1987.

Davis, Aeron, and Catherine Walsh. 'Distinguishing Financialization from Neoliberalism'. *Theory, Culture and Society* 34, no. 5/6 (2017): 27–51.

Dekker, George. 'Myth and Metamorphosis: Two Aspects of Myth in *The Cantos*'. In *New Approaches to Ezra Pound: A Co-ordinated Investigation of Pound's Poetry and Ideas*, edited by Eva Hesse, 280–302. Berkeley: University of California Press, 1969.

Dobran, Ryan. 'The Difficult Style: A Study of the Poetry of J. H. Prynne'. PhD diss., University of Cambridge, 2012.

Dorn, Jennifer Dunbar. '*Rolling Stock*: A Chronicle of the Eighties'. *Chicago Review* 49, no. 3/4 and 50, no. 1: Special issue, *Edward Dorn, American Heretic* (Summer 2004): 152–9.

Dorner, J. A. *History of Protestant Theology, Particularly in Germany: Viewed According to Its Fundamental Movement and in Connection with the Religious, Moral, and Intellectual Life.* Vol. 2. Translated by George Robson and Sophia Taylor. Edinburgh: T. and T. Clark, 1871.

Fleet, Kenneth. 'The Bank of England Takes a Neutral Stance'. *The Times* (London), 12 May 1987, 21.

Fusek, Lois, trans. *Among the Flowers: The Hua-chien chi.* New York: Columbia University Press, 1982.

Hall, Matthew. *On Violence in the Work of J. H. Prynne.* Newcastle upon Tyne: Cambridge Scholars, 2015.

Hall, Stuart. *The Hard Road to Renewal: Thatcherism and the Crisis of the Left.* London: Verso, 1988.

Halliwell, James Orchard. *The Nursery Rhymes of England.* London: Frederick Warne, 1886.

Haviland, Julian. 'Break in Talks Pleases Tories'. *The Times* (London), 22 February 1985, 1.

Healy, Pat. 'Health Service Told to Cut More Jobs'. *The Times* (London), 23 August 1983, 1.

'Managers Refuse to Suggest Victims'. *The Times* (London), 23 August 1983, 2.

'Patient Care and Facilities Certain to Suffer, Embattled Regions Say'. *The Times* (London), 22 August 1983, 4.

Helm, Alex. *The English Mummers' Play*. Woodbridge and Totowa, NJ: D. S. Brewer and Roman and Littlefield, 1981.

Herbert, George. *The Temple: Sacred Poems and Private Ejaculations*. Cambridge: Thomas Buck and Roger Daniel, 1633.

Horsnell, Michael. 'Threat to Baby in 6p Mugging'. *The Times* (London), 22 August 1983, 1.

Husserl, Edmund. *Cartesian Meditations: An Introduction to Phenomenology*. Translated by Dorion Cairns. The Hague: Martinus Nijhoff, 1960.

'Impressive Start by New CE Heath Management'. *The Times* (London), 22 May 1987, 24.

Jeschke, Lisa. 'Late Early Poetry: A Commentary on J. H. Prynne's *Unanswering Rational Shore*'. *Hix Eros* 4: Special issue, *On the Late Poetry of J. H. Prynne* (2014): 61–76.

Julian, John, ed. *A Dictionary of Hymnology: Setting Forth the Origin and History of Christian Hymns of All Ages and Nations*. New York: Charles Scribner's Sons, 1892.

Katko, Justin. 'Relativistic Phytosophy: Towards a Commentary on "The *Plant Time Manifold* Transcripts"'. *Glossator: Practice and Theory of the Commentary* 2: Special issue, *On the Poetry of J. H. Prynne* (2010): 245–93.

La Berge, Leigh Claire. *Scandals and Abstraction: Financial Fiction of the Long 1980s*. Oxford: Oxford University Press, 2015.

Lander, Richard. 'The Technology That Had to Come'. *The Times* (London), 27 October 1986, 31.

Lapavitsas, Costas. *Profiting without Producing: How Finance Exploits Us All*. London: Verso, 2013.

Latter, Alex. *Late Modernism and* The English Intelligencer*: On the Poetics of Community*. London: Bloomsbury, 2015.

'Liffe Trading Almost Doubled Last Year'. *The Times* (London), 12 May 1987, 21.

Lintott, Wayne. 'Shareholders Fear 1984'. *The Times* (London), 25 August 1983, 14.

Livingstone, Ken. 'Monetarism in London'. *New Left Review* 137 (January/February 1983): 68–77.

Luna, Joe, ed. *The Letters of Douglas Oliver and J. H. Prynne, 1967–2000*. Amsterdam: The Last Books, 2022.

MacKenzie, Donald. *An Engine, Not a Camera: How Financial Models Shape Markets*. Cambridge, MA: MIT Press, 2006.

Mao Tse-tung. *An Anthology of His Writings*. Translated by Anne Fremantle. New York: New American Library, 1954.

Mathewson, G. F., and R. A. Winter. 'The Economics of Vertical Restraints in Distribution'. In *New Developments in the Analysis of Market Structure: Proceedings of a Conference Held by the International Economic Association in Ottawa, Canada*, edited by Joseph E. Stiglitz and G. Frank Mathewson, 211–39. Cambridge, MA: MIT Press, 1986.

Mellors, Anthony. *Late Modernist Poetics: From Pound to Prynne*. Manchester: Manchester University Press, 2005.

Milton, John. *Poetical Works*. Edited by Douglas Bush. London: Oxford University Press, 1966.

Mullan, John. 'Prynne's Progress'. *The Guardian* (London), 24 February 2004. www.theguardian.com/books/2004/feb/24/poetry.news.

Nienhauser, Jr., William H., ed. *The Indiana Companion to Traditional Chinese Literature*. Vol. 1. Bloomington: Indiana University Press, 1986.

Oliver, Douglas. *The Diagram Poems*. London: Ferry, 1979.

Oliver, Paul. '"Beating the bounds": Switching Boundaries over Five Millennia'. *Traditional Dwellings and Settlements Review* 15, no. 2 (Spring 2004): 7–17.

Pardo-Guerra, Juan Pablo. *Automating Finance: Infrastructures, Engineers, and the Making of Electronic Markets*. Cambridge: Cambridge University Press, 2019.

Patterson, Ian. '"Fool's Bracelet"'. *QUID* 17: Special issue, *For J. H. Prynne, in Celebration* (2006): 50–2.

Pattison, Neil, Reitha Pattison, and Luke Roberts, eds. *Certain Prose of The English Intelligencer*. Cambridge: Mountain, 2012.

Phillips, Pearson. 'The Sound of Money'. *The Times* (London), 29 April 1987, 14.

'Taking Stocks to Stores'. *The Times* (London), 28 April 1987, 12.

Phillips and Drew advertisement. *The Times* (London), 14 October 1986, 22.

Poole, Teresa. 'NFC Board Seeks Flotation Mandate'. *The Times* (London), 12 May 1987, 19.

Potter, Robert. *The English Morality Play: Origins, History and Influence of a Dramatic Tradition*. London: Routledge and Kegan Paul, 1975.

Pound, Ezra. *The Cantos of Ezra Pound*. New York: New Directions, 1996.

The Translations of Ezra Pound. London: Faber and Faber, 1970.

Prynne, J. H. 'China Figures', review of *New Songs from a Jade Terrace: An Anthology of Early Chinese Love Poetry*, trans. Anne Birrell. *Modern Asian Studies* 17, no. 4 (1983): 671–88.

Field Notes: 'The Solitary Reaper' *and Others*. Cambridge: privately printed, 2007.

'Keynote Speech at the First Pearl River Poetry Conference, Guangzhou, China, 28th June 2005'. *QUID* 16 (February 2006): 7–17.

'A Letter to Andrew Duncan'. *Grosseteste Review* 15 (1983–4): 100–18.

Letter to the editors. *Rolling Stock* 8 (October 1984): 2.

'Mental Ears and Poetic Work'. *Chicago Review*, 55, no. 1 (Winter 2010): 126–57.

The Oval Window: A New Annotated Edition by N. H. Reeve and Richard Kerridge. Hexham, UK: Bloodaxe Books, 2018.

Papers. University of Cambridge Library.

Poems. Hexham, UK: Bloodaxe Books, 2015.

Word Order. Kenilworth, UK: Prest Roots, 1989.

Raine, Craig. 'All Jokes Aside'. *The Guardian* (London), 11 March 2008. www .theguardian.com/books/2008/mar/11/poetry.thomasstearnseliot.

Reeve, N. H., and Richard Kerridge. *Nearly Too Much: The Poetry of J. H. Prynne*. Liverpool: Liverpool University Press, 1995.

Roberts, Luke. *Barry MacSweeney and the Politics of Post-War British Poetry: Seditious Things*. Cham: Palgrave Macmillan, 2017.

Routledge, Paul. 'Walker Rules Out Talks As Miners Vote to Strike On'. *The Times* (London), 22 February 1985, 1.

Ruggles, Wesley, dir. *I'm No Angel*. Hollywood, CA: Paramount Pictures, 1933.

'Shares of the Cake'. *The Times* (London), 27 April 1987, 1.

Smith, David. 'Industry Investment Dips by 3%'. *The Times* (London), 22 May 1987, 23.

Sutherland, Keston. 'Hilarious Absolute Daybreak'. *Glossator: Practice and Theory of the Commentary* 2: On the Poetry of J. H. Prynne (2010): 115–47.

'J. H. Prynne and Philology'. PhD diss., University of Cambridge, 2004.

Tate, Michael, and David Smith. 'Shares Peak on Poll News'. *The Times* (London), 12 May 1987, 19.

Thatcher, Margaret. 'Interview for *Sunday Times*'. *Margaret Thatcher Foundation*. www.margaretthatcher.org/document/104475.

United Kingdom. *Parliamentary Debates*, Commons, 13 July 1983. https://api .parliament.uk/historic-hansard/commons/1983/jul/13/death-penalty.

Vogl, Joseph. *The Specter of Capital*. Translated by Joachim Redner and Robert Savage. Stanford, CA: Stanford University Press, 2015.

Wagner, Richard. *Tristan und Isolde (Tristan and Isolda): Opera in Three Acts*. New York: Fred Rullman, [ca. 1890].

Walter, Timo, and Leon Wansleben. 'How Central Bankers Learned to Love Financialization: The Fed, the Bank, and the Enlisting of Unfettered Markets in the Conduct of Monetary Policy'. *Socio-Economic Review* 18, no. 3 (2020): 625–53.

Ward, Daniel. 'Day Calls for Morals in Business'. *The Times* (London), 22 May 1987, 25.

Ward, F. W. Orde. *'Twixt Kiss and Lip; or, Under the Sword*. London: Gardner, 1890.

Wilkinson, John. 'Heigh Ho: A Partial Gloss of *Word Order*'. *Glossator: Practice and Theory of the Commentary* 2: On the Poetry of J. H. Prynne (2010): 295–325.

Wilson-Smith, Peter. 'Lowest Exports This Year Put Britain in the Red'. *The Times* (London), 25 August 1983, 1.

'Wilting Lilley Aims for Revival'. *The Times* (London), 12 May 1987, 20.

Yeats, W. B. *The Collected Plays of W.B. Yeats*. London: Macmillan, 1966.

Acknowledgements

I am indebted to Eric Falci for his incisive editorial suggestions and to John Wells, Senior Archivist at the Cambridge University Library, for his generous and invaluable assistance in facilitating access to the relevant files in Prynne's papers. I am also grateful for the careful attention and helpful suggestions of two anonymous reviewers and for feedback from James Garwood-Cole, Kirsten Ihns, and the University of Chicago Poetry and Poetics Workshop, November 2021. My thanks to J. H. Prynne for permission to quote his poems.

Cambridge Elements ≡

Poetry and Poetics

Eric Falci

University of California, Berkeley

Eric Falci is Professor of English at the University of California, Berkeley. He is the author of *Continuity and Change in Irish Poetry, 1966–2010* (2012), *The Cambridge Introduction to British Poetry, 1945–2010* (2015), and *The Value of Poetry* (2020). With Paige Reynolds, he is the co-editor of *Irish Literature in Transition, 1980–2020* (2020). His first book of poetry, *Late Along the Edgelands*, appeared in 2019.

About the Series

Cambridge Elements in Poetry and Poetics features expert accounts of poetry and poets across a broad field of historical periods, national and transnational traditions, linguistic and cultural contexts, and methodological approaches. Each volume offers distinctive approaches to poems, poets, institutions, concepts, and cultural conditions that have shaped the histories of poetic making.

Cambridge Elements ≡

Poetry and Poetics

Elements in the Series

Theresa Hak Kyung Cha in Black and White
Josephine Nock-Hee Park

Somewhere Else in the Market: An Essay on the Poetry of J. H. Prynne
Joe Luna

A full series listing is available at: www.cambridge.org/EIPP

Printed in the United States
by Baker & Taylor Publisher Services